Made to Worship

A Spiritual Enrichment
Journey and Journal

Lora Hurd Griffin

PRESS

www.xulonpress.com

It is a privilege and honor to endorse *Made to Worship* by Lora Hurd Griffin. It is a reality statement on bringing rituals and routines into authentic worship. There is obvious passion to worship God in spirit and in truth (John 4:24) throughout this book. The spirituality that is presented is more than mere words. It is a lifestyle. The compassion she has for the Word of God can only come from having a serious personal relationship with Jesus. I highly recommend this book for enhancing and empowering Christian personality and relationships, the Church, and the Community through authentic worship. The standards and steps for accountability to worship should challenge all who read this to make authentic worship a mandate to their daily living.

—Rev. Dr. Bishop E. Carter III

Pastor, Bethsaida Baptist Church, Lexington, KY

Moderator, Consolidated Baptist District

Association of Kentucky

Director & Faculty member, Simmons College of Kentucky

Chief Chaplain (Retired), Kentucky Dept. of Corrections

5th District Chaplain, Omega Psi Phi Fraternity, Inc.

(KY/Tenn.)

Made to Worship by Lora Hurd Griffin is a series of study for the new Christian and a revisit for the seasoned Christian. Twenty-one days of comprehensive study that gives the reader the opportunity to respond and reflect on each topic. This highly recommended and thoughtful piece of writing is thorough and complete.

Rev. Ralph E. Johnson

Presiding Elder, African Methodist Episcopal Church

Dedication

～～～

T here are several to whom I dedicate this book: to my parents-Robert L. and Ruthy M. Hurd, who first taught me the love of Christ and portrayed God's love in their daily living, and to my siblings- Barbara, Robert L. II, Bobby, and Licia- who demonstrated love in action. This is to my husband and best friend- Ron-who is always supportive and keeps me grounded and mindful of God's Word, and to my children-Yavon, Dionne and Latoyia, and son-in-law, Chris Weathers- who even now continue to carry the banner of Christ and the message of love in their lives. And finally, to my grandchildren who are now learning of Christ and the lessons of love being lived before them. My prayer is that they also fully learn to worship Christ as He desires and makes worship a part of their lifestyles.

Acknowledgements

~~~

First of all, I thank God for His divine inspiration and guidance in the creation of this book. There would be *no* book without Him. Thank you to my friends, family and pastor-Rev. Richard Gaines, and special friend, Rev. Dr. Bishop E. Carter III- who helped read and critique my first writings and/or offered words of encouragement. Thank you to Preeti Voshi, who designed the burning and committed heart for my graphic illustration. I offer a special thank you to Dr. Vanessa Jackson, who read, re-read and assisted in so many ways; to the Women's Ministry Leadership Team of Consolidated Baptist Church (Anita Bradley, Carmen Webb, Jessica Coffie, Jovanna Atkinson, Meladee Evans, and Vel Williams) who loved me enough to embark on the initial journey as a group study, and to Sis. Sarah Gaines for her approval of the Women's Ministry study. God bless you!

I can't thank you all enough for your time, early morning study sessions, efforts and love. Please know I am eternally grateful. And finally, a sincere and gracious thank you to Mr. John Townsend, and Presiding Elder Ralph Johnson, who so generously offered personal critique, encouragement and feedback to ensure the Word of God was being presented accurately. Simple words cannot express how much I appreciate all that you have done to make this work a success. Thank each and every one of you from the bottom of my heart. Let us all continue to be the worshippers that God desires.

Table of Contents

~~~

Preface

∿

Worship is simple-and yet complex. Like a gleaming diamond of great worth, worship is very multifaceted. It requires more than the surface attention most of us tend to render.

It is much more than simply going to church and engaging in the routine and rituals of church service. Worship is action. It is the process of continuing the work God designed for us to do.

True and authentic worship is a lifestyle. It is the preeminent focus on Jesus in our thoughts, words and deeds. It begins in the heart and encompasses all that we do for the glory of God.

This exploration attempts to highlight a number of those facets so that we better understand our role and responsibility as worshippers.

This is more than simply a book to read at your leisure. It guides you in better understanding what true worship really is. It implores you to search and evaluate yourself to discover where you are in your worship life and prods you to enrich your worship of our Almighty God. It impels you to strengthen your relationship with and worship of Christ, and inspires you to get up off of those pews and get to work for Him. True and authentic worship is work! It is love in action!

Each section will ask you to examine yourself. I strongly urge you to deeply reflect on each reading, deliberately pause and meditate on the questions, and seriously consider the implications for further advancing your worship life. Write your thoughts in the journaling space provided. Search for and partner with a confidant with whom you can discuss your intimate revelations and who will help hold you accountable for boosting your worship to the next realm. Accountability promotes commitment. Spiritual growth and Christian maturity is developed through relationships, open discussions, and expanding your understanding of God's Word.

By the end of this 21-day inner journey you will better understand what God's desire is in worshipping Him in spirit and in truth. You will better understand how the many facets of worship come together to create the magnificent jewel that God desires. Achieving this introspection will help you greatly enhance your worship life. It will ignite your desire to give more than lip-service and Sunday-morning praise to the Lord our God.

Why 21 days? It has been said that anything done in 21 days will become a habit. Let this be the beginning of your new habit of truly worshipping God. Develop a lifetime disposition of being a worshipper.

I challenge you to be honest with yourself and be honest with God. Learn to worship Christ as He desires. Learn to be a true worshipper. Don't just read the book, study it! Dig deep into yourself and become a better ambassador for Christ. Learn to truly worship Him in spirit and in truth. Make a commitment to yourself and to God to be more intentional in your efforts to glorify Him and to edify the body of Christ.

Your life has an eternal purpose. We were made to worship!

Introduction

∿

Welcome Saints!

Whether you are new to the body of Christ, are Christian babes moving towards spiritual maturity, or seasoned saints, our primary goal, as adopted children of the King, is to bring honor and praise to God. The Bible tells us:

"[God] predestined us to be adopted as His sons through Jesus Christ, in accordance with His pleasure and will – to the praise of His glorious grace, which He has freely given us in the One He loves... in order that we, who were the first to hope in Christ, might be for the praise of His glory."[1]

This exploration has been designed so that we might learn to more fully worship God.

Maybe you're a mature Christian and you feel this book is not for you. But you probably know someone that may benefit from its reading. Maybe you're not quite as mature in your spiritual growth as you desire. Then I pray that you might find a nugget or two that may help stimulate your growth in Christ, for He wants us to mature in His knowledge and wisdom so we can bear better witness of Him. Either way, if you've chosen to read this book I hope you might share it with someone else. Help to spread God's gospel and the benefit of knowing what our primary purpose is here on earth with someone who may not fully understand the foundational reason we are here.

My prayer is that you will all find some small gem of wisdom; some thought that creates an "Aha" moment- a spark of enlightenment, a lifting of the spirit- as to our principal purpose and calling. After all, I was made to worship! You were made to worship! We were made to worship Jesus the Christ! May God grant you that nugget, that portion, that small something that speaks to your soul, and may the song of praise permeate your heart and mind until you continuously sing in glorious fullness to God – "I was made- to worship, I was made- to worship, I was made- to worship you!"

To God be all glory, power and honor! Amen.

-L

Day 1

Welcome to the Kingdom!

∿

"The Lord is my strength and song, and He is become my salvation…"

(Exodus 15:2, KJV)

Congratulations! Giving your life to Christ is the absolute best decision that you will ever make. You were made to be a worshipper, and Christ welcomes you!

May I ask –are you new to the kingdom of God or are you one who is already a member? Are you associating with a new body of believers? Or are you, perhaps, one who accepted Christ some time ago, have been attending a local church and are now ready to take your worship to the next level?

Did you ever stop to ponder just why you joined the church in the first place? Were you running from something

– some bad experience you realized you had to get away from, some negative "something" that was ruining your life and the lives of your loved ones? Was it some indescribable "evil" that had taken over your very person, your very essence? Were you searching to fill some all-absorbing emptiness you couldn't explain? Searching to resolve some wrenching pain you just couldn't take anymore? A spiraling sense of "lostness", of hopelessness so deep you couldn't rip it out? What was it? Were you finally drawn to decide you've had enough, that it was time to find a better way? To look to Christ for answers? Did you realize there was more to life than just mere existence- thinking that you were here for a reason but really had no idea of what or why? Gone astray and desperately searching for help? Grieving, hurting, and needing assistance? Perhaps, you finally understood the majestic love of God and the great price He paid for our sins and acknowledged Christ as your Savior. Whatever it was, whatever brought you to the realization that your past life had to change, that it was time to accept Christ into your life – God bless you! God loves you! And God welcomes you!

The body of Christ welcomes you with open arms! We are grateful that you heeded the loving call of Christ saying to you that enough is enough! It's time to join your true family! It is time for you to recognize your primary purpose, your prime reason for existence, your true nature in Christ. You were made to be a worshipper! And we want you to understand what that means.

Many people excitedly- and often tearfully- give their lives to Christ, join a local church body, attend worship services, and think- "my job is done. All I need to do now is continue attending church on a regular basis, give some money, participate in an activity or two every now and then (*if* I'm asked), and then try to be a good person and just coast into glory". Right? Mistake! There is much work to be done! Much to be learned! Now begins the daily, continual process of developing your new life in Christ! Growth must take place!

Just as our human body begins as a baby- small in size and stature, our new life in Christ begins as a spiritual babe- small in spiritual strength and knowledge. Just as our physical bodies require physical food to grow daily, our spiritual bodies require spiritual food for daily, steady growth. As we learned to crawl before walking, to say simple words, phrases and sentences before talking, and to learn our alphabet and then words before reading, so too must the spiritual person within us learn to grow in Christ. It doesn't just happen.

It is a process that takes time, effort, and study. It requires the desire to know more, to inwardly reflect and internally challenge. It entails a deeper understanding of who we are and whose we are. It leads to a heart-rending understanding of why we are here and the true purpose for our existence. Spiritual growth requires that we progress to become mature Christians the same as we must grow and learn to become mature adults.

Chronological age has nothing to do with this progression. Length of church membership alone has nothing to do with this growing process. Some physically adult members of the kingdom are spiritually infants in their Christian maturity. Why? Because they have either not realized the need, made the serious, concerted effort to make themselves available, or have not taken, been presented with or sought ever deeper, next-level opportunities to grow more fully in Christ.

You must have a desire, a thirst, a hunger to know more, and to understand the "why" behind your reason for joining the church, for joining the kingdom, for your belief in Christ. So, let's do some self-exploration as we begin to better understand our reason for being here, our reason for joining the kingdom of God.

God loves you more than you know and excitedly awaits you learning more about Him, more about your purpose for being here, and even more about you.

Why I Joined Church

Do this. Take a moment for some deep, internal reflection. Be honest! Young or old, new convert or seasoned member- why did you really join church initially? People join the church for different reasons. Did you join at a young age because your friends were doing it, your parents made you, or some member of the church thought it was time and encouraged you to do it? Did you join as you got a little older because the music was great, and you felt comfortable within the confines of that setting? Were you older still, ready to settle down, and came in looking for a mate? Or perhaps you envisioned taking advantage of some networking opportunities because your boss or an officer of your company attended there and you thought that would be a great political move? Maybe your love for Christ and the realization of His great sacrifice drew you to the cross. Your ability to honestly acknowledge why you joined the church will help you develop your growth plan. It will help you pinpoint and understand where you are or where you started in your spiritual development and determine what progress has been made to this juncture. It will also help as you begin to establish how to achieve next level spiritual growth and authentic worship of Christ.

Examine yourself. Answer these three questions. Write your answers in the space provided.

1) Why did you really join church and become a member of the kingdom of God?

_____

_____

_____

_____

_____

_____

2) What do you believe about Christ?

_____

_____

_____

_____

_____

_____

3) What do you believe about being a member of Christ's church, and what does that really mean to you?

_____

_____

_____

_____

_____

_____

Day 2

God's Great Love

~~~

"For God so loved the world that He gave His only begotten Son, that whoever believes in Him should not perish but have everlasting life."

(John 3:16, NIV)

S alvation is personal.

Our relationship with God is personal and unique to each of us. There is an old saying that declares, "God protects all babies and fools." We have all been foolish during many points in our lives – done foolish things, made bad decisions, put ourselves in compromising situations that we knew were not good for us; things that could have cost us our health or our very lives. Yet, we did them anyway. When we think back over all the things God has already protected and delivered us from- dangers seen and unseen, we should all shout – "Thank you Jesus!" When we reflect upon where we could be today and how God has blessed us in spite of our misgivings and our wrong doings, we should all lift our hearts in praise and yell – "Thank you God!"

Your experiences, trials and tribulations are different from mine. My hurts, disappointments and circumstances are certainly different from yours, but we should all praise God for what He has allowed us to conquer and overcome. Only God knows the true depth of our sin, and only the blood of Christ can cleanse and remove the stain of our transgressions.

God gave His only Son-Jesus Christ- to redeem us, and to free us from our sins! Jesus came to love, heal and forgive. He came to atone for sins committed. He went to Calvary and was crucified. He gave His very life on the cross that we all might have the right to live eternally. There was nothing simple or trivial about what He did for us! He died an excruciating death for our sakes. He suffered, bled and died that we might have eternal life. That was no small thing! Despite what we've seen depicted in pictures, He didn't have small building nails pounded in His hands and feet as they stretched Him on the cross. Those were thick iron pegs! He was lifted up as a sin-offering for what we would do and have done. He voluntarily gave His life and His blood as a sacrifice that we might live with Him forever. He died so we could be reconciled back to His Father. He didn't have to die- He *chose* to die -for us.

But He didn't just die and it was over. Thank God that was not the end! Christ rose from the grave on the third day with all power in Heaven and Earth in His hands that we might be raised with Him in glory. He lives today with His Father in heaven and has prepared a heavenly home for those who believe in Him. And that's not all! The Bible emphatically says- "He is coming back to redeem those He has saved" [1]. What love! Would you have done that for persons who didn't believe in you, who didn't love you? Would you sacrifice your life for those who didn't appreciate you or the efforts you'd taken to save their lives? For those who thought your ways were too inconvenient, too hard, or seemed foolish? For those who didn't and don't even understand what real love is all about?

The truthful answer is- "no". None of us probably would. But Christ did! Therefore, we owe Him such a huge debt- *HUGE*! Ephesians 2:4-10 NIV proclaims-

"But because of His great love for us, God, who is rich in mercy, made us alive with Christ even when we were dead in transgressions[sins]- it is by grace you have been saved. And God raised us up with Christ and seated us with Him in the heavenly realms in Christ Jesus, in order that in the coming ages He might show the incomparable riches of His grace, expressed in His kindness to us in Christ Jesus. For it is by grace you have been saved, through faith- and this not from yourselves, it is the gift of God- not by works, so that no one can boast. For we are God's workmanship, created in Christ Jesus to do good works, which God prepared in advance for us to do."[2]

Christ died for all of mankind – all men, all women, and all children. Not just for a small segment, but for all of mankind, denominations aside. You do realize the "kingdom of God" is not just any one specific denomination, right? The Bible states –

"You are all sons of God through faith in Christ Jesus, for all of you who were baptized into Christ have clothed yourselves with Christ. There is neither Jew nor Greek, slave nor free, male nor female, for you are all one in Christ Jesus.

If you belong to Christ, then you are Abraham's seed, and heirs according to the promise."[3]

We are further taught- "Have we not all one Father? Has not one God created us?"[4] "...even if there are so-called gods, whether in heaven or on earth (as there are many gods and many lords), yet for us there is one God, the Father, of whom are all things, and we for Him; and one Lord Jesus Christ, through whom are all things, and through whom we live."[5] For "there is one body and one Spirit, just as you were called in one hope of your calling; one Lord, one faith, one baptism; one God and Father of all, who is above all, and through all, and in you all."[6]

Isn't it great to know there won't be just Catholics or Protestants, Baptists or Methodists, or whatever religious denomination you might belong to in heaven? And get this- there won't be any one "race" in heaven either- but "every kindred, and tongue, and people and nation" (Revel. 5:9)! [7] Every people of every color and nationality- who earnestly and fully believe- and accept- that Jesus Christ is the Son of God and our risen Savior will abide with God in His kingdom forever! How magnificent is that?! All of us! Isn't God an awesome God? An all-inclusive, awe-inspiring God!

Perhaps you are not yet a member of God's kingdom, and someone decided to share this book with you. No problem! It is never too late- while you still have breath- to give your life to Christ and to begin finding the answers to a God-focused life.

As we've often been taught and have shared with others, becoming a member of the kingdom is simple. It's like ABC –

Acknowledge you are a sinner and ask forgiveness for your sins.

Believe that Jesus Christ is the Son of God; that He died for, forgives and cleanses you of your sins.

Confess this belief with your mouth and you shall be saved.

Romans 10:8 and 9 verifies - "'that if you confess with your mouth, "Jesus is Lord", and believe in your heart that God raised Him from the dead, you will be saved."[8] It is as simple as that. But, it must be an *honest and sincere* confession of faith. When you present yourself to God in that manner, there is no waiting period, no eligibility or probationary standards, no character review, no whatever- you are saved!

Will you do that now? Jesus is waiting- just for you!

Once saved, it is then wise that you join up with a local church so you can be around like-minded, blood-saved followers in order to grow in wisdom and strength according to God's Word and learn to worship Him as He desires.

So what now? Where do you go from here? Have you thought about your next steps to become more like Christ, or is it simply enough for you to just join the church? That was a big step, no doubt! A glorious and mighty step! But is that it?

Eternal life is a gift you cannot buy in any store, at any price, no matter how much money you have or who you are. Do you realize how valuable that gift is? How can you possibly thank God sufficiently for that? Or do you feel you have accomplished your goal and settled your debt by merely giving your life to Christ? Do you think there's nothing else to be done but perhaps attend church regularly and be a good person? You became a new creation when you gave your life to Christ. But Christ expects more of you than to just sit down on the job. There is growth that must take place. There is work that must be done. The new creature in you must go through a molding process, and that process will be personal and unique to you. As we get started, let's continue our personal reflection.

A moment of reflection! Again, think deeply about the decision you've made. If you didn't do it earlier, go back and write down why you decided to give your life to Christ so you can clearly answer this for yourself. This is a moment of truth between you and God. You should fully grasp why you joined the body of Christ.

What would be your statement of witness- your testimony- to those who ask why you joined the church? You can't witness to what you don't know. Write it down in the space below. Then, use this statement as a witness to others who are unsaved. And if you begin to falter, revisit and review your reason(s) for giving your life to Christ.

_____

_____

_____

_____

_____

_____

_____

Day 3

A New Creation

~~~

"Therefore, if anyone is in Christ, he is a new creation; old things have passed away; behold, all things have become new."

(2 Corinthians 5:17, NKJV)

B ecoming a new creation begins on the inside.
While teaching Vacation Bible School, our teaching team experienced a young boy that acted up terribly in class everyday-I mean *every* day! At the conclusion of one of our daily sessions and after reassembling in the main sanctuary, this youngster got up from his padded seat and went before the waiting congregation to give his life to Christ. We were all so excited! Another soul had been saved! However, immediately upon returning to his seat, he went right back to

being the same noisy, misbehaving child he had been before presenting himself before the church.

You might wonder, "Had the lessons really reached him? What did he actually believe in his heart and why did he really go forward- as a dare? Because some of his friends decided to present themselves to Christ? For the attention and praise he thought he would receive?" We can't judge him nor speak against any inward change that must have taken place. We heard his whispered words of belief in Christ, but his unruly behavior and disruptive actions made you at least recognize that no immediate outward conversion had taken place. There certainly was no instantaneous transformation – his body didn't change, there was no realignment of his head and body parts like in the movie- *The Transformers*. There was nothing that immediately changed this kid into a mild mannered, soft-spoken, Bible-toting ambassador for Christ. With this confession occurring during the middle of the Vacation-Bible-School week, there were no baptisms that night. Had there been and he was baptized, without knowing the transforming power of Christ, perhaps you would have wondered if he hadn't gone in the water as a dry devil and simply come back up as a wet one!

Man cannot judge whether this youngster had or had not been touched spiritually to give his life to Christ; only God can do that. In fact, we cannot judge the lives of any person. We can only give witness to the fruit they bear. As Christians, our job is simply to plant the seed of God's love and His promise of restoration. We are to nourish those seeds with the water of God's Word, and pray that God flourishes in the lives of nonbelievers that they may someday give their lives to Christ. At the appointed time, God will give the increase.

Thankfully, God is the ultimate judge- not man. He is the only fair and righteous judge! God's changes begin first on the inside- within the heart. It is a heart thing!

Salvation is immediate. It then manifests itself in our outward behaviors as we grow in Christ, and learn to abide by His commandments and follow His ways. When we truly give our hearts and souls to Christ, we become new creatures; our sin-drenched souls become completely new in the Lord. We become new spiritual beings in Christ. Paul explains this conversion by stating- "therefore, if anyone is in Christ, he is a new creature; old things are passed away; behold, all things are become new" (2 Corinthians 5:17).[1] In other words, as born-again believers in Christ, we spiritually become brand-new people on the inside. We are re-created in union with Christ. We are reconciled to God the Father and begin a new life in Jesus. We are regenerated and transformed.

This regeneration, this spiritual transformation, is a gift. It is not by anything or any good works that we have done. Paul reminds us in his letter to Titus, that we are saved "not by works of righteousness which we have done, but according to His mercy He saved us, through the washing of regeneration and renewing of the Holy Spirit" (Titus 3:5).[2] This regeneration and renewal requires growth to take place. It is a lifelong process.

Reflect for a moment. Answer these questions:

What does true conversion and growing in Christ look like for you? What do you expect?

_____

_____

_____

_____

_____

_____

_____

What do you think others expect of you? More importantly, what does Christ expect of you?

_____

_____

_____

_____

_____

_____

Is this "new life" really going to make a difference in your lifestyle? In your behavior? How does this "new life" display itself on the outside?

_____

_____

_____

_____

_____

_____

_____

_____

_____

Pause and write down your honest thoughts. No one is here to judge you. We can't. The important thing is that you honestly and earnestly put on paper your true thoughts of what growing in Christ looks like to you so you can visualize and put your arms around the genuineness of your situation. Then God can begin to work with you and work in you. The great thing about Christ is that He will meet you exactly where you are.

Pray to God for understanding and growth to take place. Pray for the courage to candidly write your feelings and beliefs. Space is provided to journal your thoughts throughout this book. I encourage you to write. Keep your book private if you must, but write!

Day 4

Growing in Christ

∽

"As newborn babes, desire the pure milk of the Word, that you may grow thereby" (1 Peter 2:2, NIV)

Once you've given your life to Christ and benefitted from the transformative and saving power of His grace, it's time to grow.

Now that you've had a chance to reflect clearly on why you joined, what you expected and what growing in Christ should look like (in your opinion, and that's what matters at the moment) - where do you go from here? What are your next steps? What will you need to do? What lifestyle differences might you need to make?

Let's focus on what you must do to grow in Christ. There will never be a time when you reach a spiritual plateau where growth in Christ is no longer needed. In fact, the moment you think you've reached the top of your learning curve and are ready to put your spiritual growth on cruise control that will be the beginning of your downfall. Ask yourself- "how much and what do you really know about Christ outside of the basics"? Some people are satisfied with just knowing and doing the essentials, and that's it. But to grow deeper and stronger in your faith and knowledge of Christ, to be able to know Him better, to worship and to serve Him more, you must continually feed on God's Word. The Christian life is one of constant growth, continuous learning, and persistent transformation. While salvation is instantaneous, becoming more like Christ is a lifetime process.

Spiritual growth, just as our physical growth, requires a plan. We must be intentional in our pursuit to grow in Christ. We must construct a strategy that will raise our spiritual development to the next level. As children, we begin our education at home with our parents learning the basics – the alphabet, how to spell our names, how to count, how to tie our shoes, etc. We then enter public, non-public, or private school and progress from one grade level to the next, ever increasing in the knowledge and understanding of ourselves and the world around us. The same philosophy holds true for our spiritual progression. We must learn the foundation for our belief in Christ, nourish our minds and hearts in the Word of God, know why there is blessed assurance in our faith, and understand what God expects of us and from us.

The way to know God and His desire for our lives is to know His Word. We must ask God to reveal His Will, His Word, His wisdom and His way. If we don't know God and His truth as revealed in the Bible, then we can't truly grow in Him and worship Him as He desires. We must petition God to- "teach me thy way, O Lord, and I will walk in thy truth...".[1] Therefore, we must have a deliberate growth plan, a plan that will increase our knowledge and understanding of Christ. Our mission should be to:

"... come to the unity of the faith and of the knowledge of the Son of God...to the measure of the stature of the fullness of Christ; that we should no longer be children, tossed to and fro and carried about with every wind of doctrine, by the trickery of men,.... but speaking the truth in love, may grow up in all things into Him who is the head- Christ..." (Ephesians 4:13-15).[2]

Examination time! Let's do a quick assessment. It is not scientific. It's not based on any formal survey. Assuming you are already saved, it's just a rough, guesstimate of where you are right now in your walk with Christ. On a scale of 1 to 10, check the box that most represents the present status of your spiritual development. Be truthful!

☐ 1- I am just getting started

☐ 2- I only attend church from time to time

☐ 3- I attend somewhat regularly

☐ 4- I attend regularly, once per week

☐ 5- I attend regularly once per week and occasionally Sunday School, Bible or small-group study

☐ 6- I attend worship service, Bible or small-group study and/or Sunday School regularly and bring my Bible to follow along with the Scriptures as the Word is being taught. I listen to and take note of the message being presented but have not developed a personal prayer or study pattern.

☐ 7- I attend church regularly and participate in some further, formal educational opportunities. I am developing a personal prayer life and taking time to study the scriptures.

☐ 8- I am developing a personal relationship with Christ. After attending worship service, Bible study, Sunday School and other formalized Christian study regularly, I work to incorporate the Word of God into my daily life and make it a priority to spend personal time with God.

☐ 9- I have developed a deep, personal and loving relationship with Christ. I regularly set aside time to continually study His Word that I might know more about Him and what He expects of me. I pray daily to understand God's Will in my life, and make myself available to be used by Him. I understand I was made to worship!

☐ 10- Christ has absolute priority in my life. I know my role as a child of God. I know I was made to be a worshipper. I study, pray and live daily by His Word. I do all that Christ asks and expects of me. Occasionally, when I do fail, I promptly ask God for forgiveness and continue my walk in His light. I consistently seek the salvation of others and share the Gospel of Christ with nonbelievers. I am always mindful to praise and honor God continuously for who He is and what He has done for me.

Any attempt to assess one's spiritual development is difficult at best. There could have easily been a lot more categories and breakdowns. The endeavor here was to keep this exceptionally simple. It is certainly not a perfect assessment. Probably not even close, but hopefully it made you think a little.

So, how did you do? If you didn't attain a 10, don't worry! None of us have actually reached or will reach perfection. In fact, Romans 3:22 tells us- "for all have sinned and come short of the glory of God". We all still have much room to grow. The true measure of growth is how our lives and our actions stack up *beside* Christ – *not* how we measure up against sinners or even other Christians. The fantastic thing about God is that He meets us exactly where we are to begin working with us and in us to start the molding process to make us more like Christ.

Let's begin our enrichment plan to expand our spiritual growth. We must better understand what true worship is and what it's not, what it means to become a living sacrifice; to understand the relationship between worship and service, being committed, and what becoming a true worshipper involves. As we begin our journey and construct our plan, let's start with the foundation- knowing our purpose. We were made to worship!

Day 5

Made to Worship!

~~~

"Now therefore our God, we thank thee and praise thy glorious name."

(1 Chronicles 29:13, KJV)

We have one vital responsibility as Christians upon which all else is based.

Numerous books have been written to identify our major purpose and responsibility. All seem to have legitimate arguments and give us significant direction. Several authors have spotlighted various things they think is the most important, but still seem to fall short in actually identifying *the* most important responsibility.

Rick Warren, author of *The Purpose Driven® Life* and *Better Together: What on earth are we here for?* identifies five purposes for which he feels God placed each of us on earth: (1) to gain knowledge of and love Christ, (2) to learn to love and fellowship with each other, (3) to grow in discipleship and becoming more like Jesus, (4) to serve God in ministry, and (5) to evangelize by sharing the Good News of Christ with others.[1] That's enough to keep us all busy for a lifetime. All of these are absolutely true. All are established by God. But there is the one that supersedes all.

So, what is that one thing? What is our one primary and vital purpose for which we were created? Easy! Christ says the most important commandment, the most vital responsibility we have as Christians is to "Love the Lord your God with all your heart and with all your soul and with all your mind and with all your strength" (Mark 12:30).[2] *That* is true, genuine and authentic worship! Therefore, our ultimate purpose- is to love, praise and worship God- all in one package! It is the triune cornerstone upon which all the others rest.

When we learn to fully love, praise and worship God to the depths of our very souls- with all our heart, with all our mind, with all our strength, with all our soul, then all of our other God-mandated duties, purposes, and responsibilities as Christians will fall in line. We will want to learn more about God, to honor and serve Him; to follow His commandments and eagerly tell others about Christ. We will fervently desire to emulate Christ, to submit to His Will, to serve Him as we serve others, and to love, fellowship with and sacrifice ourselves for Christ and His kingdom. When we learn to do that, then we will become more like Jesus and fulfill our ultimate purpose. But it all starts with the deepest love, the highest praise, and the most audacious worship of Christ you can fathom.

A quick paraphrase of a song by gospel recording artist, Myron Williams declares so eloquently- We were made to worship. Our job is to be a worshipper![3] What an awesome opportunity! What a wonderful purpose and assignment! What a privilege that is! Our supreme purpose is to praise, worship and to do the Will of God. We must ask ourselves as Myron questions- are we even worthy to raise our hands to give God worship? Have we truly opened our hearts that God might enter? Are we ready to totally surrender our all to Him? If not, we must stop and ask God's forgiveness and learn to fully submit our will and become obedient to God's Will. After all, our number one purpose on earth is to worship Him. It's not about us. It's not about leaving the church edifice feeling good because of the music, or the singing, or what was going on inside the church. It is all about Christ and worshipping and praising Him for who He is, what He has done for us, and what He has done in our lives. Worship is about thanking Him for His bountiful blessings towards us. It is all about submitting and surrendering ourselves to do the Will of God.

God's Will

How do we know what God's Will is?

The Apostle John records in John 6:39 and 40- "And this is the will of Him [God] who sent Me [Christ], that I shall lose none of all that He has given Me, but raise them up at the last day. For my Father's Will is that everyone who looks to the Son [Jesus] and believes in Him shall have eternal life, and I will raise him up at the last day".[4] In other words, it is God's Will that we all are saved and have eternal life. And it is God's Will that all who believe in Jesus Christ and are saved will never be lost again but shall be raised up (resurrected from physical death to eternal life) with Christ.

If worship, then, is about submitting and surrendering ourselves to do the Will of God- to obtain eternal life and be raised up at the last day- how do we do that? The key to doing God's Will is through making Christ the center of our life and allowing the Holy Spirit to guide us. "Doing" God's

Will is the act of obeying God's commandments; the act of doing what God instructs us to do (Numbers 23:26).[5]

Avery T. Willis Jr., in the study of *Master Life-The Disciple's Personality* shares that "doing God's Will begins when you have a vision of God and His purpose for your life, and are open to letting the Holy Spirit teach you."[6] Philippians 2:13 tells us, "It is God who works in you to will and to act according to His good purpose".[7] The Holy Spirit will reveal to you God's Will for your life *if* you will allow God to speak to you (did you catch the "if" in that sentence?). You must begin to listen for and listen to God's voice and follow His urgings. Even Christ Jesus sought God's Will while He lived on earth and did not seek to follow His own- "'My food,' said Jesus, 'is to do the Will of Him who sent me and to finish His work'" (John 4:34).[8] Therefore, our supreme purpose in life is to bring glory to God so that His name will be praised, and to continue God's work. Our development in every part of our spiritual or Christian life is directly related to our commitment to God's purpose and to our obedience in submitting to His Will.

Examine yourself. Can you honestly say that the purpose of your life is to glorify God? If not, what changes, what betterment do you need to make so that your life is truly glorifying to God and is pleasing in His sight? What changes do you need to make to truly worship God and to bring Him glory? Think about that for a moment. Then write a list of things below- at least five things- that you need to do to begin your path of identifying and learning God's Will for your life and what you can do to give God the ultimate glory.

_____

_____

_____

_____

_____

_____

Did your list perhaps include a daily time for personal devotion, prayer and Bible study? Or perhaps a deeper study of God's Word through structured classes? Did you list a renewed commitment to Christ? What about Christian fellowship retreats, conferences, or small study groups? If not, please consider adding these to your list. Perhaps, there are other ways you thought of that I have not suggested. Think about including those in your list as well.

It's not as simple as saying- "OK, I'll begin to read the Bible every day". The devil will do everything possible to keep that from happening. You will find yourself creating excuses as to why you don't have the time to read or meditate daily, why you don't need a prayer partner, or why you're too busy. You'll tell yourself you have kids to shuffle from place to place, you're too occupied with all the stuff going on in your life, the overtime on your job doesn't allow you enough free time to get involved with study; blah-blah, blah, blah, blah. But we must learn to surrender our lives and learn to do God's Will. We must make a conscious and concerted effort to learn to worship God daily- in spite of all that's going on around us, within us, or against us. We must learn to develop an "in spite-of" praise and worship, so that in spite of what's going on around us we can shout – "with my lips, I worship; with my heart, I worship; with my soul, I worship You!" When we can do that, we can truly begin to praise and worship God for who He is!

Now, that we better understand our purpose- that we are here to love, praise and worship God, what's our next step? Do you fully understand what worship truly is? Remember, we can't witness to what we don't know.

Day 6

Authentic Worship

∼∾

"Yet a time is coming and has now come when the true worshippers will worship the Father in spirit and truth, for they are the kind of worshippers the Father seeks. (John 4:23, NIV)

What God wants of this generation is real, true and authentic worship.

But what is true worship? What is authentic worship? We hear preachers preach about it. The Apostle John writes about it. Many songs are sung about it. But what is it, really? Have you ever thought about it, considered it deeply, or researched it further, or do you just take for granted that it is simply something you do when the church assembles?

Most likely, the majority of us simply take it for granted. In fact, for years I naïvely assumed it was just what I did when I went to church. Worship was merely the act of congregating with the body of believers and going through the routine practices, and the rituals and traditions that had been established- period.

So why is it important to define authentic worship? Because it is hard for us to know whether we are doing something correctly, if we are not sure what that something is. It is difficult to know if we are worshipping as God desires, if we do not understand what true worship really is and to make certain that it is what God seeks. In many churches we have been inspired to study God's Word, compelled to witness, and encouraged to work, but we have given little attention to understanding the meaning of and what's actually involved in authentic worship.

Worship Defined

As I began to dig deeply into what worship really is I found that there are almost as many definitions of worship and what constitutes true worship as there are Bible scholars. Some go into deep theological dissertations while others try to provide simple, yet intellectual and profound ideas of what worship means to them.

In *Readings in St. John's Gospel* written by William Temple, worship is defined as "the submission of all our nature to God. It is the quickening of conscience by His holiness; the nourishment of mind with His truth; the purifying of imagination by His Beauty; the opening of the heart to His love; the surrender of will to His purpose, and all of this gathered up in adoration; the most selfless emotion of which our nature is capable and therefore, the chief remedy for that self-centeredness which is our original sin and the source of all actual sin." [1]

Dr. Dan Block, former professor of the Old Testament at the Southern Baptist Theological Seminary, defines true worship as the "reverential human acts of submission and homage before the divine Sovereign, in response to His gracious revelation of Himself and in accordance with His Will."[2]

But, perhaps the clearest explanation I found that provided a profound, comprehensible understanding for me was offered by Bob Deffinbaugh at Bible.org. Here, worship is provided the working definition of: "the humble response of regenerate men [and women] to the self-disclosure of the Most High God. It is based upon the work of God. It is achieved through the activity of God [and] is directed to

God. It is expressed by the lips in praise and by the life in service." [3]

So what does all of that mean exactly? I conclude that worship is like a multifaceted diamond of supreme worth. Worship is about God, to God, by the Spirit of God through the reverent, outward praise and God-focused lifestyle of born-again Christians. The Bible says: "for of Him, and through Him, and to Him, are all things: to whom be glory for ever! Amen."[4] Therefore, it is the complete humbling of ourselves before God; the realization that we are but dust in His sight; a mere vapor. It is the lowering of self in the face of realizing that God is everything; He is sovereign. He is complete within Himself. He is the creator and maker of all things; the owner of all things in heaven and in earth; and without Him we are and can do nothing. As a result, we must willingly submit to the Lordship of God, become obedient to God's Will and His way, and become one in the purposes and manner of God (John 17:11)[5].

True and authentic worship is a melding process. It is the continual, daily blending or unification of our actions, beliefs, mindsets, lifestyle and will with that of Jesus Christ. It is the mirroring of our lives and the purpose for our lives with Christ Jesus, that we might carry out His commandments and give all praise and honor to our Father. In its simplest terms, it is reverence, honor, praise, and service blended into one entity and presented to our Almighty King.

Worship is completely God-generated and God-centered. It is born out of our love and adoration for, our knowledge and respect of, and our personal experience and relationship with God. It is our deepest, awe-inspired response to God for Him first revealing Himself to us. Worship is our response reflected through our lifestyles to the truth of God's Word which sanctifies us (John 17:17 and 19).[6]

Deffinbaugh notes, "the case is similar to that of love- 'We love Him, because He first loved us' (1 John 4:19). Love does not find its origin in man, but in God. Our love is only a response, only a reflection of God's love toward us. And so it is with worship. We worship God because He has made Himself known to us and has instructed us to worship Him."[7] God has made Himself known to us by the indwelling of His Spirit within us- within our hearts.

A State of the Heart

Based on those definitions and enlightenment, let's take a closer look at worship. True worship, then, starts with the state of the heart. It is a heart thing; and out of the heart

57

begins the authentic worship of God. When we have experienced a true and personally intimate encounter with God, when God divinely reveals to us first-hand knowledge of His character – His unconditional love, His longsuffering and patience, His compassion, His grace and His mercy- then we can begin to truly worship God for who He is. In fact, we can't help but to worship Him.

Genuine, true and authentic worship is indisputable adulation from the heart; a genuine out-pouring of our hearts to Christ. It is a heartfelt, all-encompassing focus on expressing our love to God. As illustrated in the graphic, authentic worship is a pure and humbled heart that is opened to God, the surrendering of the human will to God's purpose; our humbled response to the self-disclosure of God. It is our genuine, outward manifestation of love, praise, reverence and adulation; our personal devotion to God through an intimate relationship with Him; the surrender of our human nature to the nature and characteristics of Christ through a lifestyle that reflects God. Authentic worship is a heart burning for Christ, willing to complete the work of God by serving others and leading others to Christ. It is our humbled submission to God's Word and His ways by following His commandments, and focusing our hearts, mind, and spirit on Him. Authentic worship is everything we are and everything we do being directed to God to give Him the supreme glory and praise.

It puts me in mind of the process of developing a loving relationship with that special someone that you've met. As feelings begin to develop for that person, you have a burning desire to be around him or her more. You want to constantly be in their presence, to spend valuable time with them, to know more about them, talk with them; to share information about each other; to intimately be in their company.

Learning to authentically worship God has a number of similar aspects. True worship is about being in love with Christ. In Mark's letter to the Christians in Rome, as quoted earlier, Christ tells us we must: "Love the Lord your God with all your heart and with all your soul and with all your mind and with all your strength" (Mark 12:30).[8]

As our love for Christ grows, as we begin to truly worship God, we should want to know more about Him, yearn to be in His presence, long to talk to Him, experience Him, and to search for Him. We should desire to become more intimate with Christ, to move our relationship to the next level. Not much different than how we would cultivate a lasting relationship with anyone else we truly cared about- our boyfriend, girlfriend, our spouse, children, or family. The more we begin to learn about God, the more we should want to know Him; the more we should want to worship Him and let Him know how much we love Him. Our hearts should constantly burn for Christ.

We should excitedly await time to be in His presence-communing with and longing to be filled with His Spirit! Diligently seeking to be in His company! Hebrews 11:6 says that "He is a rewarder of them that diligently seek Him."[9] When we seek Him with our whole hearts, we are then rewarded through the magnification of the intimate, loving relationship we so desire.

As there is no structured pattern for falling in love, there is no rigid formula for worship; no ordered or prepared outline that I can lay out for you. That is because worship is a function and condition of the heart. It is personal and unique to each individual.

God cares about and thoroughly examines the state and condition of our hearts. Worship is about a surrendered heart, a heart of humility. It is an all-encompassing surrendered love that is offered to God. It is empowered by the Spirit of God, and outwardly manifested through the personal devotion and professed praise of the individual to God. Psalm 9:1 says – "I will praise thee, O Lord, with my whole heart."[10]

Worship then is engaging the whole heart in honest and reverent praise to our Savior and Redeemer. True worship is learning to worship God as He desires- in spirit and in truth.

Examine your heart. Obviously, you can't look at your physical heart, but let's explore what God might think about the state of your heart. This will take some serious internal reflection and prayer. Ask yourself:

1) Are you truly in love with Christ- have you fully surrendered your heart to Him? _____

_____

_____

_____

_____

2) What actions have you taken to get to know Christ better; to develop a more intimate relationship with Him?

_____

_____

_____

_____

_____

_____

3) Do you look forward to spending quality time with Christ?

_____

_____

_____

_____

_____

4) Do you tell Christ you love Him on a regular basis?

_____

_____

_____

5) List what can you do to improve your relationship with Him?

_____

_____

_____

_____

_____

_____

_____

_____

Write down your answers. Then pray and ask God to reveal to you the true condition of your heart and how your love and worship of Him can be better expressed in your behavior.

What is Authentic Worship?

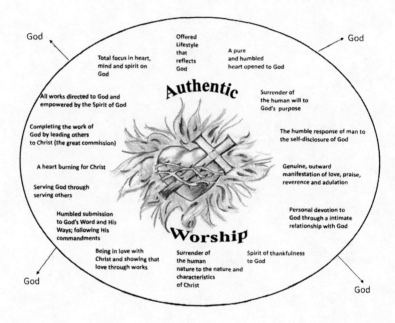

God

Offered Lifestyle that reflects God

A pure and humbled heart opened to God

Total focus in heart, mind and spirit on God

God

Authentic

Surrender of the human will to God's purpose

All works directed to God and empowered by the Spirit of God

Completing the work of God by leading others to Christ (the great commission)

The humble response of man to the self-disclosure of God

A heart burning for Christ

Serving God through serving others

Genuine, outward manifestation of love, praise, reverence and adulation

Humbled submission to God's Word and His Ways; following His commandments

Personal devotion to God through a intimate relationship with God

Worship

Being in love with Christ and showing that love through works

Surrender of the human nature to the nature and characteristics of Christ

Spirit of thankfulness to God

God

God

The Committed Heart drawing by Preeti Joshi,
University of Kentucky

Prayer Reflection

What has God spoken to you in your prayers?

_____

_____

_____

_____

_____

_____

_____

_____

What did you say or promise to God?

_____

_____

_____

_____

_____

_____

_____

Day 7

Worshipping in Spirit

~~~

"God is spirit and his worshippers must worship in spirit and in truth."

(John 4:24, NIV)

True and authentic worship- worshipping in spirit, is paying sincere and reverent respect to the One who created us.

Worshipping God in spirit is doing so deeply and sincerely from the heart without deceit or chicanery. To worship God authentically, you must fully honor and value God simply for who He is- period! Not for what God can do for us or what God can provide for us or anything else that is 'me" focused. We *do* want to recognize and thank God for what He's done, but we must first honor Him for who He is.

For a number of Christians, unfortunately, "the concept of worship has been diluted to mean the designated period during which they come together in corporate assembly to sing songs, praise (or quietly observe others praise), and get temporarily excited about the Lord."[1] I say 'temporarily" because some of us seem to lose our "religion" and the spirit of worship just as soon as we leave the doors of the sanctuary. The devil intervenes and somehow their worship and Christian attitudes get left inside the building.

Regrettably, more and more of worship has become something we do once or twice a week (on a good week) to pay homage to God, to momentarily focus on Jesus Christ, to seek personal gratification for our dutiful resemblance of obedience, or to absolve one's guilt for the lifestyle we've lived throughout the rest of the week. Many of those who errantly slip into this category think the more they can work themselves into an emotional state of accord ("being in the spirit") by allowing the music, and private or public prayers to achieve a state of worshipful bliss, the more they can nullify what they are doing when they are not corporately "worshipping" or daily obeying God in their lives.

Psalm 29: 2 tells us to –"Give unto the Lord the glory due unto His name; worship the Lord in the beauty of holiness."[2] Worshipping in spirit- with your spirit in union with Christ-has nothing to do with us. It has everything to do with Him. It is simply about the glory and honor that is due Christ because He is holy and worthy to be praised. Our worship of Christ should not be conditioned upon what He has done or will do for us- but to honor and praise God for who He is and Jesus' gift of salvation.

The Bible says: "God is Spirit, and those who worship Him must worship in spirit and truth"[3]. But "worshipping in spirit" is more than just Sunday morning praise or revival-roused emotionalism. Worshipping God "in spirit" means with reverence and attentiveness; honoring God for the right purpose with devoted singleness of heart, mind and soul. It is the filling of the human "temple", the unifying of the spirits (of God and man) by the Spirit of God. It is not prefabricated. It is not coerced, forced or faked. It is not something we can turn on and turn off at our discretion.

I remember during a very emotional service, a young woman exuberantly yelled, cried, danced and swayed in the aisles of the church. The ushers on duty quickly came over to ensure the young woman didn't hurt herself or anyone seated close to her. In physical exhaustion, the young woman collapsed. The ushers fanned her until she was restored. Immediately after her episode when the woman regained her composure, she looked over and nudged her friend and laughingly said something like- "girl, did you see me get filled with the Holy Spirit? I was all over the place. I was about to tear this place apart, so I had to get myself together". Upon hearing this, I was absolutely dumbstruck! I questioned to myself, did the Holy Spirit have her acting like that or did she generate that response herself for the attention and comments she would receive from her friend? Was she in control or was the Spirit guiding her actions? Was she simply aroused by emotionalism or was she allowing the Spirit to have His way?

A similar experience was witnessed while observing a videoed service at a small, country Pentecostal church. As the minister intensely evangelized the congregation following a couple of song selections, a few gentlemen arose from their seats or other places within the sanctuary (almost as if on cue) and began to briskly run about the church. After encircling the sanctuary a few times while the minister continued his sermon, one of the men ran towards the baptismal pool, bouncingly hesitated for a moment, and then plunged head-first into the still collection of water before exiting the pulpit. A second man whipped his suit coat over his head several times before landing it on the head of the passionate preacher as you could hear those recording the service chuckle a bit in the background. While we can't judge whether or not the Spirit was working in any of these people, their seemingly orchestrated actions might cause some pause and reflection and make you think– uuummmmmmm!!!

Worshipping 'in spirit' doesn't put you out of control; rather, it puts you under the control of the Holy Spirit. It is giving our full, reverent, undivided, and respectful attention to God. Every act of worship within the assembly of believers should be for praising and glorifying God, and for the uplifting and spiritual building of the saints. In order to properly worship God in spirit and with the right attitude, we must take time before entering into worship to ensure our hearts and emotions are in line with Christ so that we are in the proper frame of mind. We should become one with Christ in mind and spirit, as if no one else was in the room but you and God.

Rick Warren states- "worship is your spirit responding to God's Spirit. God designed your spirit to communicate with him."[4] Thus, worshipping in spirit is the complete interlocking of your heart and spirit with God; totally centered on God and in union with God as the Holy Spirit reigns. When we worship in spirit, our spiritual antennas are alert to God so that we are in tune to Him and can hear what He is saying to us. We are open to receiving His Word, and attentively listening for His Voice.

True and authentic worship-worshipping in spirit- is solely directed to the Father; it speaks of the characteristics of our God. It is not for the entertainment of observers. It is born of heartfelt reverence and deliberate, intentional praise to God. It is a thankful response for what God has done for us. It is not a repayment for what He has done, however. We can't repay Him. We can't be good enough. We can't give enough. We can't do enough, or love enough or anything else enough to repay God for His goodness, His mercy, and His grace. True and authentic worship of Christ is our response, our offering back to God for His undying love to us.

Worshipping in spirit- is a person's Holy Ghost-generated, heart-quickening response to God for the indwelling of His Spirit within us. It is worship that glorifies God.

1 Corinthians 6:20 says, "For you were bought with a price; therefore glorify God in your body and in your spirit, which are God's."[5] For that reason, we are not to take lightly that which should be considered serious. Worship to God is

71

holy. Our character and actions, our act of reverence, must also be holy. In 1 Peter 1: 13-16 we read,

"Therefore, prepare your minds for action; be self-controlled; set your hope fully on the grace to be given you when Jesus Christ is revealed. As obedient children, do not conform to the evil desires you had when you lived in ignorance, but just as He who called you is holy, so be holy in all you do; for it is written: Be holy, because I am holy."[6]

While we cannot say how anyone will honestly react to the stirring of the Holy Spirit within them, it is something that we must take very seriously. We must allow the Spirit to lead us and not attempt to direct our own actions. Perhaps, we should ask ourselves – is the Holy Spirit really guiding me or is this self-contrived? Am I responding to the indwelling of the Spirit or am I simply performing for those around me?

We must remember the prime purpose of our worship is to honor, praise, exalt and glorify God for His grace in freeing us from the bondage of sin.

True and authentic worship is the act and mindset of praising God at all times. God is Spirit. He is not limited to one place and time- such as worship service on Sundays or other designated times during the week, or on special planned occasions. God is omnipresent, ubiquitous and universal. He is everywhere at the same time and can be worshipped everywhere and at all times; not just during the assembling of the church. And yes, you *can* worship alone as I have heard some argue as their reason for not attending church. You can worship outside while viewing nature (although I think that professing to be able to worship while on the golf course may be stretching it). While we are not limited to where we choose to individually worship, the Bible *does* instruct us to not forsake the assembling of ourselves together (Hebrews 10:25).[7]

It is not where we worship that counts, but *how* we worship and *who* we worship. Therefore, it is critical that we take the time before we worship-wherever we are- to ensure our hearts, minds and emotions are in the proper disposition. Again, John the apostle tells us we *"must* worship in spirit and in truth" (John 4:24).[8] This is not optional. It is the Master's mandate. It is the only way that is pleasing and acceptable to God- the ultimate authenticator of true worship.

Reflection time. Do this. Take time to really think about how you respond to the music and the sermons particularly during your time of corporate worship. View this in your mind – like mentally rewinding a movie. Write your answers below. Be candid with yourself and transparent with God. This is ultimately between you and Him. Discussing your thoughts with others, however, helps you to confront your reality and confess your shortcomings. Then pray and ask God to let your actions, your behavior and your spirit be led at all times during your corporate and private worship by the power of the Holy Spirit alone.

Now answer these four simple questions:

1) Is your response truly generated by the Holy Ghost stirring within your heart or simply to the rhythm of the music or the energy in the room?

_____

_____

_____

_____

_____

_____

2) Is your response inspired by the people around you?

_____

_____

_____

_____

3) Would your reaction be the same if no one was in the room but you?

_____

_____

_____

_____

4) Are your actions or utterances actually being directed towards God to give Him praise and glory or so that those around you know you are "in the spirit"?

_____

_____

_____

_____

_____

Day 8

Worshipping in Truth

~~~

"And you shall know the truth, and the truth shall make you free"

(John 8:32, NKJV)

God is truth, and the source of all truth.

True worship must be based on the truth of Scripture, and "grace and truth came through Jesus Christ" (John 1:17b).[1]

God wants us to know the truth about Him. He wants us to not just talk about His goodness from a distant, impersonal viewpoint, but to fully understand and grasp His majesty, His holiness, His omnipotence, His omniscience, His love, His longsuffering, His mercy, and His truth. Worshipping in truth is gaining a crystal clear comprehension of God's glory and His grace. It is seeing the condemnable condition of ourselves in the light of God's truth, and enabling His truth to penetrate our hearts, convict our spirits, save our souls, and direct our lives.

Worshipping in truth means to intentionally and continuously strive to learn of God through His Word and to emulate Christ's ways. We learn God's Word by studying and meditating upon the scriptures and by praying and asking the Holy Spirit to reveal God's wisdom to us. Speaking with the Corinthian church, Paul explained that even he "did not come with eloquence or superior wisdom" but through a "demonstration of the Spirit's power, so that your faith might not rest on men's wisdom, but on God's power" (1 Corinthians 2:1, 4-5).[2] Thus, it is through the power of God and the working of the Holy Spirit that we learn the truth of God. As such, we are to fervently seek God's Word and then allow God to reveal His wisdom through attentively and intently listening to and absorbing His Word. We must search scripture, digest it, and apply it to our lives.

Knowing God's Word and not applying it to our daily lives is not worship. It is only when we know the truth of God, begin to consistently and daily incorporate the principles of God's Word to our lives that we begin to conform to His likeness and live a God-honoring lifestyle. It is when we begin to emulate His ways that we truly worship God as He desires.

Intimately understanding and personally experiencing God's character will impact our worship and our praise. True worship is based on our appreciation of who God is and who we are in Him. Many of us have only become acquainted with or have superficially learned of the concepts of God that were handed down by outside sources with little personal knowledge of our own. We fail to personally pray and study God's Word. We fall short of individually experiencing the Almighty or developing a loving relationship with Him. As a result, our knowledge of Him is weak and in some cases our personal interpretation of His handed-down Word is flawed. Paul, in his second letter to Timothy tells us to "study to shew [show] thyself approved unto God, a workman that needeth not to be ashamed, rightly dividing the word of truth" (2 Timothy 2:15).[3] Therefore, it is important that we personally study God's Word and ask the Holy Spirit to reveal its understanding that we might clearly appreciate what it means and how it specifically relates to us.

How we see and know God influences how we worship Him. Countless people fail to approach God or approach

Him in a fearful way, because their notion of God is faulty or incomplete. Further, our conflicted attitudes, experiences and misinformation about God can negatively impact and influence our relationship with and our openness towards God.

We've commonly learned or heard of God's attributes as our Father, our Friend, our Provider, our Counselor, or our Guide, but how do we personally view Him? Do we see God as a loving Father who hears, understands and forgives, or as a demanding, domineering Father who only condemns and chastises? Do we truly envision God as an intimate Friend who always looks out for our best interests or only as a casual acquaintance who has little interest in us or our issues? Do we praise God for His longsuffering and patient teachings or visualize Him as a harsh, intimidating Teacher who continuously points out our shortcomings and our faults? A loving Advocate or a wrathful Judge? A kind Counselor or a mistrustful Master? If we don't know the true character of God in the fullness of His truth, we cannot truly worship God in the completeness of His glory.

In his book, *How to Listen to God,* Charles Stanley shares that far too many people have negative ideas about God and therefore have a lackluster experience with Him. As a result, they are in emotional or spiritual imprisonment. In a story he tells about one particular parishioner, he explains how far too many believers continue to feel guilty and unworthy of being fully accepted and forgiven by God. They confess, repent, and rededicate their lives to Christ time and time again, but the same shroud of guilt seems to cover them even as they leave the altar. Many never truly understand the difference between true guilt (that stemming from sins actually committed against God) versus false guilt (that which Satan places on us by continuously condemning and convincing us that we can never live up to God's standards). When they are finally able to understand what Christ's death on the cross did for us, then they can fully be free of the burden God never intended for us to carry.[4] When we learn the truth of God, then we are truly free from the shackles of sin; free to realize the full benefit of our adoption through Christ; free to live as heirs and joint-heirs of the kingdom of God.

Satan uses false guilt to deceive and prevent us from knowing and appreciating the truth of God. When God has forgiven, we are wholly and completely forgiven. He remembers our sins no more. Our slate is wiped clean. Unfortunately, people fettered by the guilt of past sins they have not entirely released in Christ remain so focused on their faults that they fail to focus on their Savior. When we feel under such constant condemnation and neglect to comprehend the total forgiveness of Christ, we fall short of worshipping God for who He is or as He desires. According to Charles Stanley, "that's why we're not excited about Jesus Christ and why we do not glorify God to the fullest measure."[5]

Too many of us remain enslaved by Satan's false guilt because we do not know or understand the grace and attributes of God. We cannot sincerely worship God in truth because we don't know the character of God. We fail to appreciate His love and forgiveness, and therefore we can't abundantly appreciate the gift of God. Christ's forgiveness gives us freedom from sin's grasp. Through Christ, "you have been set free from sin and have become slaves to righteousness."[6] Jesus tells us –"I am the way, the truth, and the life. No one comes to the Father except through Me" (John 14:6).[7] Therefore we cannot know and worship God in a manner that pleases Him except to know His Son- Jesus and to learn from His teachings. And we cannot amply praise and glorify God as He deserves until we can comprehensively understand the truth of God and the depth and breadth of His forgiveness.

God loves us dearly and wants us to know Him profoundly. Thus, we must pray and ask God to teach us to truly worship Him according to the truth of His Word. If we don't know the truth, we cannot worship in truth. When we know and abide by God's enduring truths; when we are able to recognize and appreciate the full splendor of God and glorify the full character and completeness of God, we can't help but to worship Him.

True worship is Christ-centered. It is rooted in the character of God and based on the truth of His Word.

Examine yourself. Think deeply on these questions and then journal your responses below.

1) How do you view God? Describe your relationship with Him.

_____

_____

_____

_____

_____

_____

_____

2) How has or how could an incomplete or distorted view of God's character impact how you worship Him?

_____

_____

_____

_____

_____

3) How can a more profound knowledge of Christ's nature make you free to worship Him more abundantly?

_____

_____

_____

_____

_____

4) In what ways do you strive to emulate the character of God?

_____

_____

_____

_____

_____

Day 9

God-centered Praise

～～～

"I will praise [thee], O Lord, with my whole heart; I will shew forth all

thy marvelous works."

(Psalm 9:1, KJV)

One of the greatest mistakes in our generation is making worship man-centered.

It is the Holy Spirit that works within us to enable us to worship. It is the truth of God's Word that compels us to keep our focus centered on Christ. All praise should center on God's character, His power, His promises, His provision, His love, His forgiveness, and His sacrifice.

When our worship is reduced to how *we* choose to offer praise and what keeps us entertained, we are creating a self-centered focus- putting our attention on the desires of the flesh- not in God. Psalm 22:25 clearly directs the single-mindedness and the object of our praise affirming - "My praise shall be of You [God] in the great assembly."[1] Nothing else. Praise that is solely directed to Christ is God-centered praise.

Regrettably, we have gotten so caught-up in centering our attention on the interests and comforts of man- the music played and songs sung, the repetition of catchy phrases, the emotional stirrings of our assemblies, and the creature comforts for our convenience- that we have lost focus on true worship. Our minds stay centered on earthly things, "but our citizenship is in heaven" (Philippians 3:20).[2] Thus, our focus must be directed to our Father. Our hearts and our praise must target Christ. While the repetition of the speaker's phrases might be a resourceful tool for creating emphasis on what is being said, mindlessly reiterating catchy phrases is of the flesh. It is hyped sensationalism. However well intended, it can easily misdirect our attention from God to man.

In some instances, we have become so focused on ensuring we project a comfortable, coffee-shop-type atmosphere for the casual presentation of God's Word that we have failed to embrace the sanctity of His Word or His place of worship. Our focus is on the comforts of man, not the fullness of God. In some large metropolitan worship centers, congregants are presented with an almost retreat-like atmosphere upon entering the facility. The various beverage stations offer a myriad of coffees, drinks, and/or juices, or hot chocolate in the winter. Other refreshment stations may offer fresh cookies. Groupings of deeply comfortable chairs arranged in sight of TV monitors provide a convenient view of the services while parishioners enjoy their refreshments without having to step inside the sanctuary. However, if they choose to venture in, all are welcome to bring their coffee and treats inside as they sit in theatre-style seats to casually observe and listen to the message being presented. The sacredness of the occasion seems lost. The reverence of the reason for assembling seemed misplaced. The misdirected focus appears to be on pleasing man more than praising God.

While God will certainly meet us where we are in our walk of faith, and although Christ invites us to "come as we are"- as empty pitchers needing to be filled, in many instances we have taken our casual comforts too far. We have ignored and misappropriated the desires of our host-God. After all, it is His house we are entering. Rather than drawing potential converts with the Word of God and for the praise of God, we strive to attract possible members with the comforts and desires of man.

Setting the atmosphere for the Holy Spirit to dwell among us and leading others to engage in true worship is about deliberately pointing all attention to and towards God. It is to enable worshippers to magnify and praise the marvelous works of Christ; not to highlight a hyped ambiance or casual countenance to satisfy the cravings of man.

Authentic Christ-centered worship is sacred. The exercise of that worship is learned. Our ability to worship is developed through the application of God's Word through trials and experience. Intentionally reflecting on how God has personally allowed us to weather our storms and overcome our tests provides us a genuine testimony. A deep reflection of how Christ has covered us in the midst of our tribulations and delivered, protected and provided for us enriches our worship. It provides an opportunity to share with others the provisions of God, to extol the power and faithfulness of Christ, and profess the fulfilled promises of our Redeemer. It affirms the realization of His truth, and affords us first-hand knowledge of God's character. God-centered praise ultimately directs all honor, glory and reverence back to Him.

Learning to respond positively in Christ-centered worship versus bemoaning difficult circumstances will help us to grow in our trust and relationship with God. And yes, many times not bewailing dire circumstances may be much easier said than done-*much easier*. But, we must stay focused on God's providential care and love for us. We must know in the depths of our hearts that in spite of whatever we must go through, God is an awesome God. He is an omnipotent God, and He alone is worthy of all honor, all glory and all praise!

Philippians 4:4 tells us to "rejoice in the Lord always."[3] Our praise of God should not be dependent on whether things are going right for us at the moment, on whether we have the house we want, the car we want, the job we want or any of the material things we want. Let's be clear. We *should* praise Him for all the material and physical blessings He has bestowed on us. But most importantly, we should praise and worship Him for delivering us from the burden of sin through the death of Jesus Christ on the cross. My pastor once exclaimed- "authentic worship is present rejoicing with future ramifications". In other words, we should learn to worship God and rejoice now for what we know God can and will do in the future, but especially for who He is.

Authentic worship is God-centered, not man-centered. I can't say that enough!

When our worship is to please God instead of ourselves, then our praise will become more meaningful and spiritually uplifting. Our worship will then become more pleasing and acceptable to God. It will become the kind of worship He seeks.

God-centered praise should be an honest expression of our love, our thanks and our devotion to our Almighty God, Jesus the Christ. Nothing else! No one else! All focus, all attention, all direction should be on drawing closer to God and drawing God closer to us.

We must be careful. Sometimes our minds and hearts are not even fully on God as we mindlessly glide through the motions of praise. We sing the songs (or just follow along), we stand, we sit, and maybe even kneel before God, but our thoughts are far from Him. Our thoughts are on other things. Our minds are cluttered with worldly concerns. We inadvertently squeeze God out. Earthly concerns take preeminence. We are not focused on Christ alone; sometimes we are not focused on Christ at all. We attend worship services out of habit, tradition, or other motives. This is not worship. In the recorded words of Matthew, Jesus cites "these people honor Me with their lips, but their hearts are far from Me" (Matt.15:8).[4] Where is your heart? Where is your focus? What is taking pre-eminence during your "worship"?

Authentic God-centered worship is more than just going through the motions. We must be diligent to ensure our hearts, minds and focus are stayed on God as we spend time communing with and worshipping Him. We must consciously devote our attention to God- actively talking with Him in prayer, intently reading His Word, and fervently listening to the Word being preached. When we claim to honor God with our hearts, while our actions and minds are focused on other things, our perceived act of worship means nothing. Simply attending church and exhibiting a posture of praise is not authentic worship.

The ability to worship God in His fullness should be every Christian's passionate pursuit. Christ-centered worship allows our spirits to form a spiritual link with God so that He can pour Himself into us and we can be filled by Him. Authentic Christ-centered worship brings us into the presence of God that we might bask momentarily in His glory. What a blessing we miss when we fail to praise and worship God as He desires. And oh how easy it is for us to fall into the arena of entertainment when we lose that focus!

When we focus on God's provision, His promises, and His power, we will worship Him as He desires. We will envelope Him with our praise. We will thank Him and praise His glorious name for being a strong and mighty God; our worship will be God-centered!

Examine yourself. Deeply reflect on and respond to these three things:

1) What things tend to easily pull your focus away from Christ? What captures your heart, your eye or your mind?

_____

_____

_____

_____

_____

2) Identify what attributes attracted you to your present location of worship. Was it solely the Christ-centered worship and the praise-centered atmosphere, or the contacts, comforts, amenities and technology the facility offered?

_____

_____

_____

_____

_____

_____

Finally, (3) list four specific things you will do going forward to ensure God's praise stays at the center of your attention.

_____

_____

_____

_____

_____

_____

Day 10

True Worship or Zealous Entertainment?

∿

"For I bear them record that they have a zeal of God,

but not according to knowledge."

(Romans 10:2, NKJV)

T rue worship is not entertainment.

There appears to be a misleading attitude engulfing many church-goers today that the purpose for attending church is to walk away personally satisfied and feeling good about simply attending the worship service and what took place in the service- rather than our *need* as born-again believers to assemble together to praise and worship God in unity. Worship is not about going to church just to have something to do or to boast we've attended. It is not for our entertainment.

While we *should* feel good about hearing a word from God, being in His presence, receiving direction and guidance for our lives, and being reminded how good and gracious God is - we must be careful of our purpose and motive for attending and participating in worship.

If your focus is on having a good time while in service, then you might need to check your motives.

The Right Motive

Self-centered motives are inappropriate and not of God.

Are you assembling with the church to worship or to be entertained? Sometimes we fall short in finding satisfaction with the worship service because our emphasis and focus is not on the proper object of our worship- God. In fact, some people move from church to church because they are looking for the wrong thing. Their hearts are not centrally focused on Jesus.

More and more people today merely want to leave the church emotionally satisfied with the spirit-rousing music, the poetic, "make-me-feel-good" preaching, the worldly antics being brought into the church or their "at least I made the effort" attitudes forgetting the real reason for coming together.

While great singing can certainly enhance the worship service, the purpose of the music and singing is to set the tone of our praise. It is to prepare our hearts and minds to receive the Word of God that we might learn more of Him, and to usher the Spirit of God into our presence.

Much of worship today has digressed to become no more than orchestrated entertainment for the masses. In some venues, we want to boogie in the choir stands and in the congregation. I'm not saying, however, that God is looking for dull and lifeless worship. Throughout the Bible, and particularly within the Psalms, we are told to make a joyful noise unto the Lord. Psalm 33:1, 3 instructs us to "sing joyfully to the Lord....and shout with joy."[1] Psalm 47:1, tells us to "Clap your hands, all you nations; shout to God with cries of joy."[2] And Psalm 98:4, 6 insists that we "burst into jubilant song with music; with trumpets and the blast of the ram's horn- shout for joy before the Lord, the King."[3] However, we must be careful to realize that there is but a thin line between true worship and high-spirited, zealous entertainment.

True and authentic worship is to be holy and sacred. It is not fabricated. It is not drummed up. It is not for public exhibition to be seen by man. The sacredness of true worship must not be sacrificed on the altar of entertainment.

During a music workshop I attended a few years ago, the visiting lyricist and choir director was busy teaching his songs and explaining the motivation and impetus behind the words to his various compositions. He taught the importance of music within corporate worship - how the singers and musicians are responsible for directing the flow of the congregants' praise and worship- and how he used his music to commune with God; how he earnestly sought God to lift him to the next realm of worship. I was profoundly inspired and moved. I anxiously looked forward to the next night of class so we could continue to learn to worship God through our music and singing.

On the second evening of our workshop as we began to prepare for our culminating concert, this same director began to teach the corresponding movements to accompany one of his songs. Now, I was good until we got to that part. Earlier he had talked about how God inhabits the praises of His people, and then he was teaching how our movements and handclapping in a self-encouraging show of excitement should stir and guide the congregation, stating "if we didn't clap for ourselves, the congregation probably would not clap for us either".

He proceeded in teaching the words to the song, and then added –"now follow me. At this part we clap, and clap; and stomp, and stomp; now sway to the right, and sway to the left, and sway to the right again, now bow, and pause, and lift back up, and clap, and clap, and stomp and stomp....". While choir members struggled to get the beat and the choreography correct, the focus on worship seemed to disappear from the rehearsal and an orchestrated practice for an entertaining performance took its place. Granted, this was a rehearsal, but all of the spirit of worship during that particular time seemed to evaporate from the sanctuary as the choir laughed at missing the beat, stomping at the incorrect time, and failing to pause appropriately so that we might clap on command. We lost focus on the beautiful, sacred words of praise the song was constructed to convey and to whom we were to direct our worship. The ushering in of the Spirit of the Lord temporarily took a back seat.

I can't speak for anyone else, but my worship and all reverence regarding our purpose in leading people in true worship was momentarily lost. I began to wonder if our structured focus on the choreography would cause the same effect on those coming to experience the culmination of our clinic. I questioned- would we be leading worshippers in actual worship or would we simply be entertaining attendees who came out to view a performance? Yet, I am quick to admit, God is a God of order. We never want to present ourselves in any manner that redirects one's focal point from Christ to chaos. We cannot lose our focus!

I am also reminded of an incident which occurred several years ago that clearly seemed to place entertainment as one key focus of the service. While attending a convention in Los Angeles with my husband, we attended a large, very widely renowned church. We were invited and accompanied by a friend and his wife who had family in the area. After awaiting the dismissal of the prior service, we were ushered into the edifice and directed to the available area for seating.

We had heard much about this congregation and of the prominent members who worshipped there. Obviously, the reputation and eminence of this church was internationally known. There were a number of "tourists" – with cameras clicking and eyes wide open in excited anticipation- from various parts of the world.

Our friend, who is the pastor of an African Methodist Episcopal church outside of Nashville, Tennessee, was asked to join the other ministers in the pulpit. The rest of us sat dutifully on the pews to which we were directed. As we sat prayerfully preparing our hearts to hear the Word of God, we listened to the devotional songs of praise and observed the beautiful stained-glass windows in the attractive edifice.

Just prior to the host pastor approaching the rostrum to deliver his sermon, the choir began to melodically sing "it's gonna rain, it's gonna rain, you better get ready and bear this in mind. God showed Noah the rainbow sign. He said it won't be water, but...." As I prepared my lips to sing "fire next time", the choir broke out in an abbreviated chorus of the 1970's pop music group-The Ohio Player's- rendition of F-I-R-E! And the music and bee-bopping was on! The choir was dancing and the whole congregation seemed to be swept away in the beat and the heat of the moment. I couldn't concentrate on what the pastor was preaching for fear that the fire was sure to come in any minute! It appeared our pastor friend didn't know whether to rock with the rest of the pulpit or run for cover! Cameras were clicking away and video recorders were capturing every scene!

While there is absolutely nothing wrong with lively and spirited music, we must not forget the sacredness and reverence of our praise. There is a delicate divide between delivering lively, uplifting, and legitimate songs of praise, and wittingly adding a stimulating rhythm to religious-sounding words that are mostly directed to or about man. We must be careful that our songs of praise honor and glorify God. Legitimate songs of praise uplift and tell others primarily of the wonders of God, not simply the on-going plight of man.

To pervert and corrupt true worship with entertainment, to have a focus on what we can get out of the service, or on how to engage congregants in a musical performance within the service, rather than directing the genuine praise to be rendered to God is an exercise in futility. It is an attempt to please and gratify ourselves. That is nothing short of irreverence and disrespect for God!

Entertainment within worship must not become a drawing card for believers and non-believers to attend church. It must not become the center of our attention, or the object of our affection. If we are to be true worshippers, we must be heedful to keep our focus and our worship singularly on Christ Jesus alone, not on Christ Jesus- and....

We must not make entertainment within the church into a small god. Exodus 34:14 reminds us "for thou shalt worship no other god, for the Lord, whose name is Jealous is a jealous God."[4] Our worship should reflect a healthy balance.

There are times when we should be reflective and serious in our worship (Exodus 19:14)[5], and there are certainly times we should show great enthusiasm and jubilation as noted in the many scriptures quoted.

In other instances, our reduction of worship may take on a completely different angle. In one major metropolitan community church, staging props which make up the "pulpit" area change with each new sermon series, and their annual Christmas "play" has grown into a professional theatrical performance with something new added each year- as if to outshine the presentation from the year before. While the message of the birth of Christ remains the central theme of the production, the fame of their eye-catching props and staging seem to draw more anticipation and reflection for some than the story of Jesus' birth being told. Some lose sight of the worship opportunity and see only the performance.

What are we going to church for? We should be congregating to collectively praise God as one voice, one body in Christ. But, if our focus is more on the rhythm of the music versus the words of praise to God, if we are drawn more to the dramatic presentation that stimulates our senses more than the Word that convicts our souls, or if we yearn more for a snazzy "show" rather than a sin-illuminating service, then perhaps we have become an audience of Christian spectators and religious thrill-seekers. We have fallen short of true worship. We have removed God as the center of our focus. We have reduced the obedient worship of God to our own self-centered amusement.

The devil knows our weaknesses and what can easily gain the spotlight of our attention. We are accountable for our actions and where we choose to focus our hearts.

The Bible does speak of singing, dancing, and handclapping as a show of adulation towards God. In fact, as the Ark of the Covenant was being brought to the City of David, King David himself danced and celebrated with exuberance in reverence to God (1 Chronicles 15:25-29).[5] Singers and musicians accompanied the procession of the ark, and all Israel accompanied it with shouts, the sounding of rams' horns and trumpets, and of cymbals and the playing of lyres and harps (1 Chron. 28, 29).[6] Psalm 47:1 exclaims "O clap your hands, all ye people: shout unto God with the voice of triumph."[7] So, the inclusion of such in our worship is not the problem. The problem comes when the focus of such dance, music, clapping or other expressions of praise directs our attention and our worship away from the Lord.

We are to make a joyful noise. But any disingenuous worship, in whatever form, ushers up false witness even though that may not be our sincere intention. We must be careful, therefore, not to pervert our worship, or that of anyone else, with anything that prevents us from sincerely and completely focusing all of our hearts, minds and souls on God. Our continual focal point must be set on the Lord. We must be mindful of our motives and our intent. We must be careful in our worship to remove anything that takes God's rightful place of preeminence. Worship is not for the purpose of finding or providing entertainment. We must be careful that our zeal is according to the knowledge and the Will of God. What's your motive for worship?

Examine yourself. I ask you to be prayerfully candid with yourself. Be transparent. Respond to the following five questions. Record your answers below. Then pray that your praise and worship be entirely directed to God.

1) What is your primary motive for attending worship?

_____

_____

_____

2) Where would God say your focus lies- on what you want to get out of the service, or what you hope to receive from Him?

_____

_____

_____

_____

3) Think deeply. While worshipping in song, which stirs you the most, the lyrics of the songs or the cadence of the music? Be honest!

_____

_____

_____

4) During worship, are you more drawn to what pulls your attention or on narrowly focusing and drawing Christ into your heart?

_____

_____

_____

_____

5) If the music wasn't great, but the pastor preached a powerful message that truly convicted and caused you to focus on your obedience to God, would you continue to look for-

ward to attending worship or would the music and singing
during the service greatly impact where you attended?

_____

_____

_____

_____

_____

_____

Prayer Reflection

What has God spoken to you in your prayers?

_____

_____

_____

_____

_____

_____

_____

_____

What did you say or promise to God?

_____

_____

_____

_____

_____

_____

_____

_____

Day 11

Make a Joyful Noise

~~~

"O Come, let us sing unto the Lord; let us make a joyful

noise to the rock of our salvation."

(Psalm 95:1, KJV)

W e are to raise our voices in sincere praise unto the Lord.

As mentioned on the previous day, the Bible clearly directs us to make a joyful and jubilant noise unto God and to sing forth the honor of His name. Psalm 81:1, exhorts us to "Sing aloud unto God our strength; make a joyful noise unto the God of Jacob"[1]; Psalm 149:3 invokes us to– "... praise His name in the dance; let them sing praises unto Him with the timbrel and harp."[2] And Psalm 150: 5, tells us to

"Praise Him with loud cymbals; praise Him with clashing cymbals."[3] God loves exuberant praise!

In a number of cases, however, we corrupt the use of music and dance, and the focus of our praise. In other instances, some of us act like we're afraid to open our mouths to praise God. Yet, Psalm 150:6, demands- "Let everything that has breath praise the Lord." [4]

Have you ever been in church where it appeared the people were reluctant to openly praise God? Where they just sat very placid and unemotional- like stones, and sounded more mournful than rejoiceful? Where they appeared afraid to say "Amen!" out loud? I have! It made you wonder if their worship was simply routine or if it was real?

I grew up in a small, conservative, mid-western Methodist church. After marriage, I joined my husband in a small, conservative Baptist church. The people of both churches were loving and affectionate folk who taught the love of God by example. There wasn't much difference in the flavor of their worship and certainly no difference in the object of their worship-Jesus the Christ. Many of the songs and hymns were exactly the same. The atmosphere was relatively the same-worshipful but often quite sober and almost dispassionate at times. I found similar environments at other churches we would visit and conjoin in worship - those predominantly black and those predominantly white. I am sure the intent was to worship God sincerely and reverently according to tradition and cultural experiences. Because of the calm and serene practices exhibited, and the very composed and solemn faces witnessed, I also learned to be very temperate and restricted in my praise.

As my husband and I visited larger, more progressive Baptist churches across the U.S., I was amazed at some of the "worshipping" we experienced. We wide-eyed observed as some members of host Baptist believers shouted, clapped, sang, danced, played the tambourine, or waved a solitary flag. I thought to myself- "this is not a Holiness church! This is not a Pentecostal church! This is supposed to be a Baptist church! What are they doing?" I was simply used to maybe a little swaying as we sang (but not too much mind you), and saying a hearty "Amen!" here and there.

I remember a lean, older, gray-haired man with weathered clothing many years ago, who would occasionally wander into one of the church services to worship. Some people thought he might have been a patient at an old mental-health hospital that resided not far from the church facility. This gentleman would slowly walk down the aisle, sit near the front of the church near the deacons, and soon loudly proclaim the goodness of God as the choir would sing and the deacons would pray. One Sunday, he was so expressive, a couple of the members decided he had to go. They attempted to call the hospital, or others that might have known him, to come and take him away from the church edifice. I prayed they would not be successful. God answered prayers, and the snowy-headed gentleman was able to continue his high-spirited and heartfelt worship. Unfortunately, after a short while, he stopped visiting our church. While some may praise God in a different manner, we are not to restrict their praise.

Another memorable person was a younger woman- although still older than me- with whom I became very close friends. She would often start talking loudly to herself in concurrence with whatever the pastor was preaching. At first, I would look at her out of the corner of my eye wondering what was going on (and others would glance at her with eyes of suspicion as well). As I came to know the chattering woman better and understood her relationship with the Lord more clearly, I then began to understand the reason behind her utterances and realized the depth of her worship. After reading my Bible and studying God's Word more earnestly, and as I developed an ever deeper relationship with Christ, the livelier my praise and worship also became.

God wants open and honest praise! We should earnestly praise God in whatever fashion is sincerely of you. We should faithfully worship Christ as the Holy Spirit directs us. Christ noted-"if they keep quiet, the stones will cry out" (Luke 19:40).[5] I don't know about you, but as I have often heard said, "I don't want the rocks crying out for me!"

Just as there are multiple attributes of God, there are many ways to express our sincere and reverent worship of Christ. We may convey our worship differently based on the diversity of our personalities and backgrounds -and that's okay. But it must be honest and genuine expressions of praise. Some may express their praise actively and vibrantly. Others may express their praise quietly and shed silent tears of joy. Some may simply rock in their seats, while others, still, may appear passive and unmoved on the outside while turning spiritual somersaults internally. The Bible speaks of rejoicing with trembling, with gladness in your heart; to praise God by singing, giving thanks, dancing, playing instruments, clapping hands, making a joyful noise, or shouting with joy. Other overt and reflective expressions of praise are also identified. Therefore, we should individually worship God with whatever expression is appropriate based on how the Holy Spirit leads and directs us personally. But, we must be certain to allow the Holy Spirit to be our guide; not ourselves, or anyone or anything else. Worship is serious. It must be sincere. It is not to be toyed with.

Since not all people express praise in the same way, we must be careful to not judge those whose expressions of praise may differ from ours. The New International Version Bible commentators shared that "even King David was willing to look foolish in the eyes of some in order to express his thankfulness to God honestly and exuberantly" (1Chronicles 15:29).[6] But be mindful. We cannot play with worshipping God and do it only for show. We must be wary that we are not reacting only to what pleases our itching ears and selfish desires, but what pleases God. Our praise must always be pleasing to God. We must remember, our obedience to God is more important that our enthusiasm (1 Chronicles 13:8-10)[7], but God wants us to make a joyful noise!

Examine yourself. Meditate and answer the following questions. Record your responses in the space provided.

1) How would you describe your praise?

_____

_____

_____

_____

_____

2) How do you think God would describe your praise?

_____

_____

_____

_____

_____

3) What influences how you praise and worship Christ?

_____

_____

_____

_____

_____

4) How do you respond to someone who worships differently from you?

_____

_____

_____

_____

_____

_____

5) What hinders you from making a joyful noise?

_____

_____

_____

_____

_____

Now, pray with me as we ask God to help us praise Him in a manner that pleases Him.

Father, there are so many carnal things that so easily hinder us from praising You as You desire. Forgive us, Lord. Help us to praise and honor You as You deserve. Help us block out the fear of being ridiculed and judged foolish in the eyes of others; let us fear only of being judged by You. Let our praise to be found worthy in Your eyes, and our hearts open to Your Spirit. Help us to realize and understand that we are all different; not all people praise You in the same manner. Let us not judge them, Father, but be respectful of our differences. Teach us to praise you with our whole hearts; to worship You fully in spirit and in truth. Teach us to make a joyful noise by the guidance of the Holy Spirit. This is our prayer, in Jesus' name. Amen.

Day 12

Be Wary of Itching Ears

～～つ

"For there are many unruly and vain talkers and deceivers, specially

they of the circumcision."

(Titus 1:10, KJV)

W e must remain spiritually alert and cautious of
what simply pleases the ear.

One of God's tools to help guide us in the teachings
and worship of Christ is the God-called and God-directed
preacher. His role in ensuring the lost are directed to God is
crucial. His voice in delivering the message of God to the
people of God is vital. But all responsibility and liability
for knowing, delivering and sharing God's Word does not
rest upon the preacher. Every believer is accountable for

knowing God's Word, for listening for God's Voice, and remaining true to His commandments.

True worship is based on our total dependence on God and His Word for spiritual guidance. We must study and know God's Word in order to stand on His truth. We must remain alert! We were warned by Paul in his letter to Titus, that there are "many rebellious people, mere talkers and deceivers" (Titus 1:10, NIV); "many insubordinate…idle talkers… who subvert whole households, teaching things which they ought not, for the sake of dishonest gain" (Titus 1:10-11, NKJV). The Bible warns that there will be those who will turn away from sound teachings; those who are easily swayed, and those who will distort the truth. Yet, we still seem to have itching ears- wanting to hear only what pleases us rather than what is faithfully taught of God.

We must carefully discern teachings that lead us to better understand and obey the Word of God, versus those which simply entertain and make us feel good. We must vigilantly learn to listen to God and lead the lost to Christ versus mindlessly being ensnared by the lure of religiously charismatic presentations. We must hunger and thirst for the truth and meat of God's Word, versus the rhyming and staging of clever phrases or the "what's-in-it-for-me" gospel of prosperity and increase. Too often I have heard people state: "boy we really had church today", but when asked what the preacher talked about, the response of many has been- "I don't remember, but the choir (or singers, whichever the case might be) really sang and the preacher really "hooped" (meaning the manner in which the presentation was delivered). My question is- were you actively and attentively listening? Were you engaged in worshipping and seeking a word from the Lord or were you simply satisfied with the entertainment value of the service?

We must be careful that we are not making the captivating and animated preacher or the emotionally stirring singing the center of our worship. We are to focus on the Word of God being preached. We are to focus on the worship of Christ. We are to focus on the message the Lord is trying to deliver to us. I am *not* saying that we should not be attentive to the preacher. Romans 10:14 asks "How then shall they call on Him in whom they have not believed? And how shall they believe in Him of whom they have not heard? And how shall they hear without a preacher?" So it is the preacher's job to present God's Word as it has been delivered unto him. Thank God for the preacher of God who tirelessly and honestly endeavors to do the work of God! Unfortunately, society has become so enthralled with the need for amusement that some preachers present God's message in a way that only actively astounds and captivates the ear, and generates the superficial responsiveness of their listeners because that's what we want. We seem to cater to, or appear drawn by that which simply delights the ear- not that which convicts the soul. It is vastly important to "have leaders who can effectively preach God's Word, but it is even more important to have [believers] who can live out God's Word and be examples for others to follow."[1]

As referenced in our opening scripture, the Apostle Paul warned Titus to be on the lookout for those who taught unsound principles and led others in error. There are some who have evil motives- pretending to be Christians as a way to get more money or to secure a feeling of power and prestige. Jesus and the apostles repeatedly warned against such false teachers. "Some false teachers are simply confused; they speak misguided opinions without first checking them against the Bible."[2] Others use only a small section of the Bible to the neglect of the whole. An ever-growing number choose more and more to soft-pedal God's Word for fear of offending those in the congregation. They no longer call sin-"sin", and share "stories" versus sharing the true Word of God to make their "sermons" more palatable to our ears and our ungodly lifestyles. They choose to share a casual and comfortable conversation with congregants rather than sharing "what thus says the Lord". They want parishioners to feel good about themselves as they exit sanctuary doors, rather than feeling good about the mercies and grace of God. But far many more, seem to fall prey to the enchantment of scratching our itching ears and directing our attention to themselves.

To help ease that itch, one interesting practice has become increasingly common. In surging numbers, worship leaders and TV evangelists alike attract great acclaim by proclaiming a certain declaration or affirmation and then instructing the congregation to "now say....." or "turn to your neighbor and say....." Dutifully, the congregants repeat whatever words or statements they have been instructed to repeat in a call-and-response sort of ritual. While the foundational message of many may be scripturally or doctrinally sound, it makes you wonder- "was the repetition simply to emphasize a point, or to point cleverly to the charismatic presence of the person?

As born-again believers we do have an obligation to witness to others and to share what Christ has done in our lives. But we are to give a true witness- not something fabricated

and trifle. We are told in Proverbs that "a true witness deliv-
ereth souls..."[3] And Jesus Himself tells us that we are to be
witness of Him throughout the world (Acts 1:8). But there is
a difference between witnessing for Christ and just mechanically repeating words or phrases that one has been instructed
to utter in obedient and robotic response.

Genuine praise and worship is not about whipping up
an emotional high or a false act of devotion, nor does it
pull one's attention from God to reiterate catchy phrases to
fellow congregants. Authentic praise needs no prompting.
When the Holy Spirit moves, prompting is not necessary.

Time and again I have observed people robotically turn
to the person or persons seated immediately around them and
repeat the instructed phrases without any real thought to what
they were actually saying. For instance, the preacher may be
saying something like "I trust! Now, turn to your neighbor
and say-trust!" The congregation mechanically repeats-
"trust!" The affirmation is positive. It seems harmless. It is
related to the sermon. We should trust God (although the
speaker doesn't say trust who, just- trust)! So, what could be
wrong? God doesn't want vain, mindless repetition! We are
to engage our minds as well as our whole hearts in earnest

worship to Christ. In speaking with the Corinthian church in reference to speaking in tongues, Paul notes:

"For if I pray in a tongue, my spirit prays, but my mind is unfruitful. So what shall I do? I will pray with my spirit, but I will also pray with my mind; I will sing with my spirit, but I will also sing with my mind" (1 Cor. 14:14-15).[4]

In other words, both the mind and the spirit are to be fully engaged in the authentic worship of Christ. True worship is not merely the sterile, unimpassioned, reserved knowledge of God's Word nor is it simply thoughtless emotionalism. We are to receive "the Word with all readiness of mind, and [to search] the Scriptures daily, whether those things [said] were so" (Acts 17:11).[5]

Be on guard! We all know Satan will use anything and anyone to deter us from fully giving God worship. He will even use ministers and ministry leaders- if he can. Pray for discernment that any orchestrated behavior is not simply man-inspired theatrics for self-glorification. Be cautious that these antics are not just to spotlight the speaker or to hype the flock.

Please understand, this is *not* to say that every minister or worship leader who uses this practice has the intent to fleece the flock or call special attention to himself or herself; most have very well-intended motives. Perhaps, some of these adroit affirmations may even help influence people to focus on the words spoken- to draw their attention back to the subject and message being presented. If so- great! Perhaps, they are an attempt to put parishioners in a frame of mind to concentrate on the Word of God. Fantastic! After all, God wants us to listen to Him. In Psalm 81, God tells Israel- "Hear, O My people...O Israel, if you will listen to Me! But My people would not heed My voice. Oh, that My people would listen to Me, that Israel would walk in My ways! " [6] But, often we choose to be more attentive to the theatrics and the music within the service rather than to truly hear what "thus says the Lord".

Be careful! We must not be drawn only to the speaker's personal wit, charm and charisma; to what sounds good. We must earnestly seek the message the Lord desires for us to hear. More specifically, we must be attentive and alert to the message He has for us individually. We must remain alert to the practices that exalt the teacher versus those that extols Christ and His righteous. We must be watchful of those things that distort the truth of God. In the Apostle Paul's letter to Timothy, he warned him that "the time will come when men will not put up with sound doctrine. Instead, to suit their own desires, they will gather around them a great number of teachers [preachers, evangelists, worship leaders, etc.] to say what their itching ears want to hear" (2 Timothy 4:3). [7] That time has come; that time is now!

Pray for insight. Pray for discernment. Truly listen to the message, not just get caught up in the heat of the moment. The atmosphere is hyped. The energy in the room is electric. The listeners are engaged, but the worshippers' focus- their "ear"- is momentarily drawn away from God to a rote repetition and exercise of repeating to their neighbors what was just said- "trust"! But trust what? Trust in what? Trust in whom? And do you *really* trust? Instead of some people earnestly testifying about their trust or belief in God, they've been naively coerced into "testi-lying" to comply with the charismatic charm of the speaker. It sounded good; the speaker said to say it; they wanted to appear in the spirit, they were excited, so they complied- whether or not they actually believed in what was being said or taught at the moment. This is mindless worship; and mindless worship is meaningless! God doesn't want the shallow repetition of words that are not offered with a sincere heart.

The sad thing is once a trendy practice like this gets started and one person receives a large congregational response to it, then other worship leaders seem to pick it up and replicate the same actions to be part of the hottest craze. They want to be "hip". However, as learned from a Scottish minister while attending a Baptist conference, "all born again Christians should strive to be 'HIP' – possessors of humility, integrity, and purity of heart". We should earnestly strive to reflect the image and characteristics of Christ. We must not be found guilty of spiritual apathy and the casual adoption of worldliness.

As we assemble, let us be careful of how our actions and activities might misdirect true worship. Let us ensure Spirit-filled praise- not man-generated emotionalism. Let us passionately focus on Christ, and fervently focus on extracting the message God has for us. Let us feverishly fight to keep God as the center of our praise. Let us ensure we reflect God in our lives and in our worship. Don't let "itching ears" pull our attention or our worship from Christ!

Examine yourself. Answer these questions. Take the time to prayerfully think about it and write your answers below. Be open.

1) Where is your attention? Are you more focused and aroused by the rhythm and rhyme of the words presented or the lessons being taught?

_____

_____

_____

_____

_____

2) Do you earnestly work to block out anything that distracts your hearing and understanding the Word of God, or are you captivated by other things?

_____

_____

_____

_____

_____

3) Identify what you do intentionally to focus on *how* the word being preached specifically applies to you?

_____

_____

_____

_____

_____

_____

_____

4) Identify four things you can do to ensure your mind and focus stays on Christ. What can you do to improve your focus on true worship?

_____

_____

_____

_____

_____

_____

_____

_____

Day 13

Do We Reflect Christ?

〜〜〜

"For whom He foreknew, he also predestined to be conformed to the image of His Son that He might be the firstborn among many brethren." (Romans 8:29, NKJV)

We are to reflect the image of Christ.

The question we must ask ourselves regarding that statement is - do we? We are responsible for the image we project to the world. How the world views us determines in large part how they view Christ. All too often, we are accused of being hypocritical in our representation and we turn others away from Christ. We must be vigilant and mindful of the image we cast.

We must be careful of the spotlights and showcases we present to the world. We must be especially careful that what we say and what we do are in alignment. We cannot extol the goodness of God while in church, and then live our lives in any ungodly manner while away from the assembly of believers. It is not enough to give lip service to our Christian faith; we must live it- daily.

True, none of us are perfect. And, yes, we do all sin. It is a battle we all must consciously fight day by day to win. It is a battle that we must hand over to the Lord in prayer for strength and guidance so that we might become more obedient to His commandments, His Will and His way of living. It is a war we must continuously engage in order to show ourselves as worthy ambassadors of Christ. But when we openly and publicly commit sins or allow others within our body who openly and publicly commit sins to then be positioned to visibly represent the church, we – the church body – give ourselves a black eye. We open ourselves to question, ridicule, and worst yet, the resulting rejection of Christ and His gift of salvation by non-believers and those who may be on the fence. We become accountable for turning a blind eye and of condoning sin. Non-believers become very quick to say-"look at them. They are no better than me. So, why do I need to be saved or join church?" That is why so many non-Christians and "not-sure-they-wanna-be" Christians look at us as hypocrites and find no liability in how they should live their lives. The Bible tells us – "be very careful, then, how you live- not as unwise but as wise, make the most of every opportunity, because the days are evil. Therefore do not be foolish, but understand what the Lord's Will is."[1] We can't provide a testimony for God when our daily lives inside and outside the church are in shameless shambles- doing everything but witnessing for the Lord.

Let me clarify. The act of joining church in itself does *not* save you. And enticing non-believers to join the church only to increase the numbers of the congregation or to feel that *we've* drawn them to salvation is *not* the goal. Encouraging them and leading them to give their hearts and souls to Christ- *is*.

Sin-confessed believers joining church is an act of obedience to God. It is the joining of a body of saved souls so we might gain strength and fellowship, and to praise God corporately or together. We are to bond in unity of spirit, with one voice to worship Christ. Only a genuine belief in Jesus as the Son of God; a belief that He died on the cross to redeem us from our sins, and the belief that He rose again from the dead- only a true belief in Christ- will save you. But be mindful, not everyone that attends church is necessarily saved. I am reminded of a good friend who shared a statement one of her sisters made to her professing – "you confuse us with Christians. We go to church, but we are not Christians." Her sisters are not alone in this ritual of simply "attending" church.

God abhors hypocrisy! He doesn't want pretentious or phony praise. God is not interested in our showmanship or our vain attempts to entertain. While we are not- or ever will be- perfect beings, and the best of our earnest attempts to worship God as He desires are not perfect, it must be sincere. But sincerity alone is not enough. Be cautious of being sincerely wrong! Sincere and authentic worship comes from the heart and is directed to God through the work and guidance of the Holy Spirit.

While "we all sin and come short of the glory of God"[2], we must not use our sinful nature and God's infallible forgiveness as an excuse for our continual and misdirecting behavior that may thwart the salvation of others. Our sinful nature desires what is contrary to the Spirit, but we cannot casually accept and adopt the mindset of- "what I do behind closed doors or in private won't hurt." We are to live by the guidance of the Holy Spirit. While we think we may be fooling others, what is done in the dark will eventually come to the light. The Apostle Paul tells us as he speaks with the Christians at Corinth, "[Jesus] will bring to light what is hidden in darkness and will expose the motives of men's hearts".[3] Therefore, let us carefully examine our motives, our actions, our behaviors, and our lives that we don't usher up false witness and false worship unto the Lord.

People watch how we live. What testimony do we give? We must ensure our overall image and our lifestyles reflect the fruit of God's Spirit: love, joy, peace, patience, kindness, goodness, faithfulness, gentleness, and self-control.[4] As representatives of Christ, we are to "live a life worthy of the calling [we] have received."[5] As a result, we are to "put to death, therefore, whatever belongs to your earthly nature: sexual immorality, impurity, lust, evil desires and greed, which is idolatry."[6] We are to rid ourselves of anger, rage, hatred, meanness, slander, filthy language, and lying. We are to "[take] off [our] old self with its practices and…put on the new self, which is being renewed in knowledge in the image of [our] Creator."[7] "For this very reason", the Bible says, we are to:

"Make every effort to add to your faith goodness; and to goodness, knowledge; and to knowledge, self-control; and to

self-control, perseverance; and to perseverance, godliness;
and to godliness, brotherly kindness; and to brotherly kindness, love. For if you possess these qualities in increasing
measure, they will keep you from being ineffective and
unproductive in your knowledge of our Lord Jesus Christ." [8]

Jesus tells us- "you are the light of the world". Therefore
"Let your light shine before men, that they may see your
good deeds and praise your Father in heaven". [9] It is our
responsibility to reflect the God-honoring image of Christ;
to reflect and to reveal the character of Christ. We are not to
distort and dissuade the unsaved from coming to Jesus.

When we accurately display the character of Christ, our
souls will jubilantly ring out the praises of God. When we
begin to imitate the life and love of Christ, we will become
a servant to man and follow the footsteps of the Master. This
is a critical part of our worship.

Examination time! Answer the following:

(1) What do you think your lifestyle and behavior says about your worship?

_____

_____

_____

_____

_____

2) Can people tell you are a follower of Christ by your lifestyle, motives and actions? How will they know?

_____

_____

_____

_____

3) Write your eulogy. Does it echo a lifestyle that reflects Christ?

_____

_____

_____

_____

_____

_____

_____

_____

_____

4) Identify four things you can do going forward to better reflect Christ in your life and lifestyle. Record your answers below.

_____

_____

_____

_____

_____

_____

_____

_____

_____

Day 14

Worshipping Through Service

∿

"I have brought you glory on earth by completing the work you gave

me to do." (John 17:4, NIV)

Service is a form of worship.

We are to "serve God acceptably with reverence and godly fear" (Hebrews 12:28).[1] Jesus stated: "if any man serve me, him will my Father honour" (John 12:26).[2] We are to complete the work He gave us to do- to lead non-believers to Christ. We are His servants. This is our purpose. This too is a facet of authentic worship.

Worship is Work

True, authentic worship involves work and service. The Hebrew term, *abad*, and its Greek counterpart, *latreuo*, captures the thought- "to work, to labor, or to serve". Hence, true worship involves working, laboring, and serving God and God's people. In fact, you can't truly serve God without serving His people.

Worship is an action word. Worship is about doing.

Service and worship are often linked together in the Old Testament. And it is no surprise that when we find Satan in the New Testament tempting our Lord to worship him (Luke 4: 1-7), he was asking the Lord to acknowledge him as sovereign and to surrender to him in service. Jesus responds to him saying, "It is written, 'Worship the Lord your God and serve Him only'" (Luke 4:8). [3]

We are to join with Christ in bringing others to salvation. Worship through service, then, involves continuing the work which Jesus conducted while here on earth. "'My food," said Jesus, "is to do the will of Him who sent me and to finish His work'" (John 4:34). [4] While salvation was finished on the cross, the work of bringing others to Christ is ours to continue. As one man while on earth, Jesus brought salvation to thousands. Yet, we are many. And to that end, Christ told us "…He who believes in me, the works that I do shall he do also; and greater works than these shall he do; because I go unto my Father" (John 14:12). [5] But we are still here. We are His hands. We are His feet. We are His chosen vessels. Our purpose is to bring glory and honor to Christ so that His name will be praised. Therefore, as worshippers, we have much work to do.

So, why are you still just sitting there Sunday after Sunday? That pew can't move. That pew can't talk or witness. It has no mouth. It has no means to bring others to Christ. It can only afford believers and non-believers, alike, the ability to comfortably sit and hear the Word of God. But the Bible instructs us to not be hearers only, but doers of His Word. In fact, James the brother of Jesus, in writing to the Jewish Christians who had been scattered because of persecution, plainly stated: "do not merely listen to the Word, and so deceive yourselves. Do what it says."[6]

In the Great Commission given to His disciples and to all confessed-believers in Christ, Jesus instructs us to "go and make disciples of all nations... and [teach] them to obey everything I have commanded you".[7] True worship, then, involves more than just sitting in the pews and listening to the pastor deliver a riveting sermon. Worship involves more than just listening to and participating in great songs of praise unto our Lord. True worship is more than just an occasional Wednesday night Bible study or evangelistic outreach. Service to Christ requires that we continue God's work. In the book of Deuteronomy, Moses asks the people of Israel, "What does the Lord your God ask of you, but to fear the Lord your God, to walk in all His ways, to love Him, to serve the Lord your God with all your heart and with all your soul, and to observe the Lord's commands and decrees…" (Deut. 10:12).[8] Further evidence of God's desire that we continue His work is recorded in John 17:18. As Jesus is praying to His Father, He states, "As You sent Me into the world, I have sent them into the world"[9] to continue the spread of the gospel. And because of Christ's great love, His sacrifice, and His intercession for us, we should want to work for Him. We should want to exclaim- "with my hands, I will worship; with my feet, I will worship, with my talents and the very essence of my being I will worship the Lord!"

Worship through service is the outward manifestation of our love for Christ. However, without God's love first in us and our open willingness to share His love with others, our service, our work, and our every effort means nothing.

Our work and our service must be offered in love. The Apostle Paul clearly tells us in a passage that so many of us know and love, that-

"If I speak in the tongues of men and of angels, and have not love, I am only a resounding gong or a clanging cymbal. If I have the gift of prophesy and can fathom all mysteries and all knowledge, and if I have a faith that can move mountains, but have not love, I am nothing. If I give all I possess to the poor and surrender my body to the flames, but have not love, I gain nothing."[10]

Therefore, true worship involves compassionate, loving service to God; a loving willingness to work for Him.

We eagerly desire to do things for the people we love. We enjoy giving them the best we can give. As parents, we often sacrifice for our children. We try to give them the best we can afford, and sometimes even those things we really can't afford. We long to send them to the best schools, buy the latest and greatest gadgets, games and toys, and even the ridiculously over-priced fashions they crave. Why? Because they are our children and we want to provide the best for them. How much more then, should we want to do for Christ if we love Him, if we honor Him, if we desire to praise and glorify Him? We will willingly sacrifice for our children, but are we willing to sacrifice for the service of Christ? What can we render? What service can we provide towards kingdom building to show our love for Jesus Christ?

What shall you render?

Psalm 116:12 asks, "What shall I render unto the Lord for all His benefits toward me?"[11] In other words, and more pointedly, how can you honor the Lord for all His goodness to you? What service can you provide to the Lord to express gratitude and give Him glory? Remember, providing your service to God is a form of worship. What talents, gifts, and abilities can you make available to help edify or build up the kingdom of God?

Every one of us can do something. Each of us has been given a talent, a gift, a skill, or some special knack for doing some task. And every one of us has the ultimate responsibility to evangelize the lost- to talk to a wayward soul about the goodness of God and help lead them to salvation.

As Christians, those talents, gifts, and abilities, those special knacks and skills were given to us to be used for the enriching of God's kingdom- His church and His people.

Too often and too easily, we do the opposite. We use our tongues and our actions to hurt and hinder rather than to help and heal. We exploit people for our advantage rather than to serve people for their benefit. We constantly ask or think "what am I going to get out of it?" versus "what can I freely give?" "How will it aid me versus how might it profit God?" We are comfortable in hearing the Word of God as long as we don't have to exercise any effort or do anything. We project a good Christian life on Sundays but easily live and cast a different image during the week. We're content with the idea of Jesus being a servant while here on earth as long as we don't actually have to put that into practice and serve others ourselves.

You have been called to follow Christ's lead and His life-style: "...the Son of Man did not come to be served, but to serve, and to give His life a ransom for many" (Matthew 20:28).[12] Christ served; therefore we must be willing to serve. We do it as a servant of God, for His glory. We do it as an example of His love. Because of Christ's mighty love for us, He freed us from the bondage of sin. Because of our love for Christ, we must use that freedom to serve one another in love and obedience to Him. These very words were echoed by the Apostle Paul in his letter to the churches in southern Galatia, counseling them saying-"You, my brothers, were called to be free. But do not use your freedom to indulge in the sinful nature; rather, serve one another in love" (Galatians 5:13).[13]

Therefore, we are to serve others to show our love and our gratitude to Christ and to glorify His name. The Bible further tells us:

"Whatever you do, work at it with all your heart, as working for the Lord, not for men, since you know that you will receive an inheritance from the Lord as a reward. It is the Lord Christ you are serving."[14]

As such, we should put aside our own interests to serve others- Christians and non-Christians- knowing that as we serve them, we serve Christ. The important thing to remember is we don't work for the praise of people. Our focus should always be on elevating Christ; on lifting Christ up for the whole world to see.

We must acknowledge God and serve Him with whole-hearted devotion and with a willing mind, for the Lord searches every heart and knows every motive behind our thoughts. We must continually remind ourselves that we were called to serve, *not* to be served. If we are to serve God, then we must serve God's people. We must use our gifts and talents to serve others with grace- speaking God's Word and drawing on God's strength. The Bible says "if anyone serves, he should do it with the strength God provides, so that in all things God may be praised through Jesus Christ" (1Peter 4:11).[15]

Reflection time! Think to yourself for a minute. Really examine your true feelings, your actions, and your life regarding your service to Christ. Make a mental note or actually jot down your answers somewhere. In fact, I urge you to physically write it down - in this book, a personal journal, a small notebook-somewhere. Again, I have left space here if you choose to write your thoughts in this book. Writing helps commit thoughts to memory and action.

Answer these questions, and really think about your answers.

1) What evidence shows that you love God? What have you done for Him lately (or those God loves), for free- expecting nothing in return?

_____

_____

_____

_____

_____

2) What sacrifices are you willing to make for Him to show your love and to edify the kingdom of God?

_____

_____

_____

_____

_____

3) What gifts, talents, abilities, skills, or special knacks do you have that you're just sitting on? How can they be used to benefit Christ and your local church?

_____

_____

_____

_____

_____

_____

_____

_____

Prayer Reflection

What has God spoken to you in your prayers?

_____

_____

_____

_____

_____

_____

_____

_____

What did you say or promise to God?

_____

_____

_____

_____

_____

_____

_____

_____

Day 15

Knowing and Using Your Spiritual Gifts

∼∾

"There are diversities of gifts, but the same Spirit."

(1Corinthians 12:4, NKJV)

Each of us has been given at least one spiritual gift. Have you ever wondered to yourself- "What are my gifts and talents? Do I even have any? What could I possibly offer the Lord?" I have.

I had always thought of myself as an "encourager" but seldom voiced that belief because I never knew it was actually "a gift". Encouraging others was just something I instinctively did. I would hear ministers and church leaders talk about spiritual gifts but never reconciled in my mind how that related to me. I thought 'spiritual gifts' were just for specially anointed people. Perhaps, you thought the same. Shortly, after becoming a member of my current church and during the new member's orientation, I was presented a Spiritual Gifts Assessment. This was the first time in my forty-plus years of church membership that I had ever been asked to identify my spiritual gifts and how they might be used for God's service. It was then that I truly learned that each of us has been given a spiritual gift by God. We just have to discover and maximize what that gift is.

There are four primary places in the Bible where spiritual gifts are clearly recorded: Romans 12:6-9, 1 Corinthians 12:8-10, 1 Corinthians 12:28, and Ephesians 4:11. These are not exhaustive lists, however. Other 'gifts' are scattered throughout the Bible.

In chapter 12 of the Apostle Paul's letter to the Christians in Rome (Romans 12), Paul tells us "we have different gifts, according to the grace given us".[1] He then identifies the following eight gifts: (1) prophesy, according to the proportion of faith [this is not just a prediction about the future, but it also means the ability to speak for God; speaking/preaching what God has said in His Word with power], (2) ministry/ serving, (3) teaching, (4) exhorting/encouraging, (5) giving/ contributing to the needs of others, (6) leadership/ruling [administration], (7) showing mercy, and (8) love without dissimulation or hypocrisy. In order words, love that is deep, genuine, pure, unrestrained, and unconditional; God's kind of love.

Although not included in most gift listings I've reviewed, Romans 12, verses 11-13 also mentions: being business-minded ("not slothful in business"), passionate ("fervent in spirit"), "serving the Lord" (specifically versus serving others), hopeful (" rejoicing in hope". However, this could also be interpreted as Faith), patient ("patient in tribulation"), prayerful ("continuing instant in prayer"- perhaps why we note some people as "prayer warriors"), and one who distributes to the needs of the saints ("distributing to the necessity of saints"; which perhaps could also fall under Giving).[2] Hospitality ("given to hospitality"), however, is generally included in most listings.

Paul further identifies another eight gifts of the Spirit as: (1) the word of wisdom [the ability to communicate spiritual wisdom], (2) the word of knowledge [the ability to communicate practical truth], (3) faith [not the soul-saving faith that is common to all Christians, but a superabundant faith; an unusual amount of trust in the Holy Spirit's power. Example: Paul writes in 1 Corinthians 13:2, "If I have a faith that can move mountains ...."[3]. Not all of us have this kind of faith. This is the gift of faith that is meant here], (4) gifts of healing, (5) the working of miracles, (6) discerning of spirits [meaning the ability to differentiate whether a person who claims to speak for God is actually doing so; who clearly sees the devil's cloak of deception and knows if one is speaking for man or an ungodly spirit], (7) the gift of tongues [that of your spirit communing directly with the spirit of God, and especially the ability to speak in different languages (tongues) that one has not formally learned or been taught, thereby witnessing to visiting non-believers who speak that language so that they can understand and might be saved] (1 Cor.14: 24-25), and (8) the interpretation of [those] tongues or languages (1 Cor. 12: 8-10). For this reason-the purpose of glorying God and bringing salvation to the lost-Paul says, anyone who speaks in a tongue should pray that he may also interpret what he says for the benefit and edification of the whole church.

In his letter to the believers at the church at Ephesus (in the New Testament book of Ephesians), the Apostle Paul acknowledges the previously mentioned Spirit-given gifts and identifies three additional endowments- (1) apostleship,

(2) evangelism, and (3) the gift of pastoring. All of these given:

"for the perfecting of the saints, for the work of the ministry, for the edifying of the body of Christ: till we all come in the unity of the faith and of the knowledge of the Son of God, unto a perfect man, unto the measure of the stature of the fullness of Christ" (Ephesians 4:12-13).[4]

In other words, these gifts are given so that the body of Christ (the church) may become mature in the knowledge and grace of God, reach unity in the faith, and be prepared for works of service and of spreading the gospel.

Some sources also identify additional spiritual gifts. These include: celibacy (1Cor.7:7, 8), martyrdom (1Cor. 13:3), missions (Eph.3:6-8), and voluntary poverty (1Cor.13:3). In other spiritual assessments or inventories, the gift of "apostle" is often combined with the gift of missions or that of being a missionary since the Greek word - "*apostolos*"- is the same as that of missionary- meaning "sent one" or "one sent with authority".

How do you actually determine your gifts? The best way is through prayer, study, self-examination, and working in various capacities within the church. Ask God to reveal your spiritual gifts and how they might be most effectively used for the uplift of His kingdom. Complete the Spiritual Gifts Assessment that has been provided in the appendix of this book. Dig deeper into yourself by doing a self-examination: what is it that you continuously find yourself doing without much thought? What is it that stays on your heart that you feel compelled to do on a regular basis? What are you naturally drawn to do? Study God's Word. What does His Word say about the gifts of the Holy Spirit, and how does that relate to you and what you find yourself doing? Complete more than one assessment to look for consistency in gifting. A number of free assessment tools can be found on the internet. Beware that assessments may vary, and no assessment is one hundred percent accurate or conclusive; all assessments have their strengths and weaknesses.

Natural talents or Spiritual gifts

All talents, skills and abilities are from God and are not unique to only the saved. Unsaved people are just as likely to be as talented and skilled as Christians. So, what is the difference between natural talents and spiritual gifts?

A natural talent, skill or ability is the result of a combination of parental genetics, exposure, development and/or training. However, spiritual gifts are Holy Spirit-inspired enablements independent of heritage or personal development.

Fred Zaspel, from the Word of Life Baptist Church, compares Greek and King James scripture to define spiritual gifts. According to Zaspel, "spiritual gifts or 'spirituals' (*ton pneumatikon*) are things characterized or controlled by the Spirit" and 'gifts' "translates from the Greek word *charisma*; the root word (*charis*) meaning 'grace'".[5] Therefore, spiritual gifts are gifts of God's grace characterized or controlled by the Holy Spirit. He further states that "...we find that spiritual gifts, then, are visible displays of service to others; a God-given ability [used] to serve the church effectively; a channel through which the Holy Spirit ministers to His church."[6] They are sovereignly given by the Holy Spirit and set apart for God's use. As such, spiritual gifts are given to God's children to be used in service to Him. They may be linked to a natural talent or ability, but in some cases worshippers may find themselves doing things they never expected.

Natural talents and predispositions are passed down to us and nurtured in our family; spiritual gifts are intrinsically given to each person by the Holy Spirit according to the attributes required to minister to the needs of Christ's body of believers. In his letter to the church at Corinth, Paul tells us "there are diversities of gifts, but the same Spirit. There are differences of ministries, but the same Lord. And there are diversities of activities, but it is the same God who works all in all" (1 Corinthians 12:4-6).[7] Although our gifts and the service we render or the ministries we serve may differ based on the gifting of the Holy Spirit, God is the source of all spiritual endowments.

Spiritual gifts are to be shared; they are not for your own self-advancement. Adrian Rogers notes in his book, *What Every Christian Ought to Know Day By Day: Essential Truths for Growing Your Faith,* "your spiritual gift is not for your enjoyment; it is for your employment. Your spiritual gift is a tool, not a toy. [They] are designed for mutual encouragement. [They] are never an end in themselves, [but] are meant to profit the entire body [of Christ]."[8] Thus, the purpose of all spiritual gifts is to edify the body of Christ-the church. They are specifically given so that you might do a job in and through the church. As adopted children of Christ, we are responsible for using our gifts for serving God and enhancing the spiritual growth of the total body of believers. They are given so that we can work more effectively as a unified body in Christ to build God's kingdom. Paul emphasizes that by stating: "to each one the manifestation of the Spirit is given for the common good" (1 Cor. 12:7).[9] Take note that Paul specifically states that each manifestation of the Spirit is given for the "common good" of the church, not the private benefit of the possessor.

The use of your spiritual gift or gifts is also a form of worship; its focus being directed to the glory of God.

The Bible decisively instructs us to "earnestly desire the best gifts" - those that are more beneficial to the entire body of Christ, and goes further to note "yet I show you a more excellent way– love" (1 Corinthians 12:31).[10] While there are many gifts, and some people may have more than one, no gift is superior to another-except love. God is love, and the excellency of love is clearly denoted in 1 Corinthians, Chapter 13, for it says that without love all else is nothing.

We can take no credit for what God has freely given to us. Therefore, to simply sit on the pews Sunday after Sunday, and live our lives day after day and knowingly not use these God-given gifts for the uplift of His kingdom is like a slap in the face- an outright defiance against God. Adrian Rogers states that "to deny your spiritual gift is not humility but unbelief and rebellion. To fail to use your gift for His body and His glory is a tragic waste. It is poor stewardship of the gift entrusted in you".[11]

We were made to worship. We were made to continue Christ's work here on earth. We were made to serve. We are to use the gifts He has given us for the building of His kingdom. As you get active in the church, your spiritual gifts will begin to surface and make themselves known to you. Put them to work! True worship is work!

Giving our bodies and our very souls to God for His use and in His worship is what God wants and expects from each of us. How about you? Are you willing to give Him your body and your soul? What about your gifts, talents and skills? What do you have a passion for doing that is just lying idle? Pray on that. What sacrifices are you willing to make for God? Ask God to search you, to strengthen you, and empower you to commit to Him your body, soul and spiritual gifts for use in His service.

Examine yourself. God will be the judge.

1) What are you doing to advance God's kingdom and the knowledge and growth of God's people?

_____

_____

_____

_____

_____

2) What are you doing to meet the needs of your local church?

_____

_____

_____

_____

3) How are you using your talents and gifts to continue Christ's work to reach the non-believer or to assist and nourish existing believers?

_____

_____

_____

_____

_____

_____

4) What more could you be doing?

_____

_____

_____

_____

_____

_____

I urge you to do five things: (1) earnestly and fervently pray that God will reveal your spiritual gifts to you, (2) complete the spiritual gifts assessment to help identify what your spiritual gifts are, (3) honestly evaluate yourself and your gifts; take time to fully understand what your gift(s) are and how God might want you to use that gift, (4) identify what you can begin to do and what you can offer as your service to Christ and His church, and finally (5) *actively* use your gifts, your talents and your skills for the advancement and growth of God's kingdom. It is only what you do for Christ that will last! Let's get to work for God! This is your reasonable service! This too is worship!

List your spiritual gifts:

_____

_____

_____

_____

How could these gifts be used and what service might you offer to Christ and your local church body?

_____

_____

_____

_____

From a larger perspective, how could these gifts be used to help build up God's kingdom and your community?

_____

_____

_____

_____

Day 16

Being a Living Sacrifice

~~~

"Therefore, I urge you, brothers, in view of God's mercy, to offer your bodies as living sacrifices, holy and pleasing to God – this is your spiritual act of worship."(Romans 12:1, NIV)

W e are to present our bodies and our lives as a living sacrifice unto God.

What do you think of when you think of presenting your life as a sacrifice? For many Christians, you may automatically go back to the Old Testament depiction of someone killing something- unblemished lambs, bulls, or rams- to make a sacrifice to God. In the Jewish tradition, in which the Apostle Paul and the rest of the New Testament writers were raised (except Luke who was a Gentile), sacrifice was an indispensable part of worship to God. And an indispensable part of that sacrifice was the shedding of blood of the animal being offered. The offering and shedding of blood was symbolic of the atonement for their sins, and affirming their relationship with God. In fact, Abraham was willing to offer the life of his own son as a testament of his faith in God. But God, satisfied with the successful testing of Abraham, provided him, instead, a ram which had been caught in a thicket (Genesis 22: 1-13).

God offered the ultimate sacrifice for the atonement of all sins by giving His only begotten Son-Jesus Christ- as a sacrifice for all. No other sacrifice of life, no other shedding of blood, can do what Jesus has already done.

As baptized believers in Christ, we have "died to sin" (Romans 6:2).[1] As stated in Paul's letter to the Romans, "we were therefore buried with Him through baptism into death in order that, just as Christ was raised from the dead through the glory of the Father, we too may live a new life".[2] Paul further notes that:

"in the same way, count yourselves dead to sin but alive to God in Christ Jesus. Therefore do not let sin reign in your mortal body so that you obey its evil desires. Do not offer the parts of your body to sin, as instruments of wickedness, but rather offer yourselves to God, as those who have been brought from death to life, and offer the parts of your body to Him as instruments of righteousness" (Romans 6:11-13).[3]

God "wants us to be transformed people with renewed minds, living to honor and obey Him."[4] Christ has already made the ultimate sacrifice through His death. Therefore, we can only offer ourselves - our gifts, our talents, our time, and most importantly our obedience- as a sacrifice to God through our daily actions and our daily lives; the daily giving of ourselves for the cause of Christ. The Life Application Bible commentators share that "God wants us to offer ourselves [by] daily laying aside our own desires to follow Him; putting all of our energy and resources at His disposal and trusting [God] to guide us."[5] We must live out our faith every day. When we sacrifice our personal desires in service to Christ, this is a form of worship. It is putting God in His rightful place of preeminence. But, we must do so willingly; no strings attached. We are not to "peddle our faith for the favors of God", as I heard one young minister say.

Being a living sacrifice is the act of giving up something we value highly for the sake of Christ. Christ gave His very life for us. Thus, being a living sacrifice for Him means devoting our lives to willingly and lovingly continue the Lord's work despite the cost or in spite of the inconvenience to us; to go out of our way for the cause of Christ.

As born-again Christians, we have been set apart for a higher calling- to do as Christ commands. We have all been called according to God's purpose, to further the building of His kingdom. When we present ourselves as a living sacrifice, we offer back to God all of the good gifts He has bestowed upon us. As part of the unified body of Christ, we are bound together and are to work collectively to bring Godly transformation to the world through the power of the Holy Spirit.

Often, we find committing our individual bodies and resources to God for His use to be a challenge. In fact, we habitually have a problem fully surrendering ourselves to God. But, God expects us to honor Him fully with our lives and not allow our flesh or sinful nature to dominate control. The Apostle Paul shares in the book of Romans how difficult it is to master the body and do those things Christ wants us to do. He writes:

"I know that nothing good lives in me, that is, in my sinful nature. For I have the desire to do what is good, but cannot carry it out. For what I do is not the good I want to do; no, the evil I do not want to do- this I keep on doing. Now if I do what I do not want to do, it is no longer I who do it, but it is sin living in me that does it. So I find this law at work: When I want to do good, evil is right there with me. For in my inner being I delight in God's law; but I see another law at work in the members of my body, waging war against the law of my mind and making me a prisoner of the law of sin at work within my members".[6]

Can you relate to Paul? I believe we all can. Pray with me right now that God will reveal those things that constantly prevent us from giving ourselves as a living sacrifice to Him:

Thank you Jesus for sacrificing Your life to pay the debt for our sins- a debt we could not pay. Thank you for loving me in spite of my sins. I ask, right now, for your forgiveness. I ask for Your guidance and help, for I can do nothing without You. Lord, I want to be used by you. I offer myself as a living sacrifice to work for You according to Your Will. I offer my heart, my mind and my body to be used by You, oh God. Search me Father. Reveal and remove those things that prevent me from giving myself wholly unto You. Strengthen me where I am weak. Help me lean not to my own strength, understanding and desires, but to surrender myself fully to You- daily- that I might be used for the uplifting of Your kingdom. Hear me, O Lord and answer my prayer. I can do nothing without you Father, for You are my strength and my Redeemer. Use me God as Your servant. It is in Jesus' name I pray. Amen.

Wait for God to reveal those weaknesses and allow Him to remove your stumbling blocks. Obey God and surrender yourself to His commands and direction.

You have an important role to play in the removal of these impediments. You do realize that, right? You have a personal responsibility. You can't just keep doing what you've always done and then say "well, I'm waiting on the Lord to remove them." You have to actively put forth a sincere and conscious effort to stop doing whatever it is that obstructs you from overcoming your specific stumbling-block. If your pitfall is procrastination, you have to aggressively work to avoid putting off those things you are reluctant to do. If your Achilles' heel is gambling, you have to assertively abstain from visiting the gambling boats; stop hanging out with those friends who so easily entice you to gamble. Instead, fix your eyes on the work God would have you to do.

God desires our show of faith. If we pray for the removal of our challenges in sincere faith and vigorously work to abide by Christ's desires, He is faithful to answer our prayers. Mark 11:24 tells us: "whatever you ask for in prayer, believe that you have received it, and it will be yours."[7] Thus, with your effort and faith, God will give you the strength to overcome and subdue whatever hinders you from making yourself available to do His work. That means you have to lay aside your excuses. Stop looking for new reasons to not work for Christ. Make some sacrifices. Change some priorities in your life. Realize life is not all about you. It is, however, all about Him!

It doesn't mean we won't fall or concede to our weaknesses from time to time. Even the Apostle Paul had difficulty in always doing what was right. We are no different. But we must be vigilant in our efforts to do what is right.

Bringing our thoughts, emotions, actions and behaviors under the power of Christ is one way that we give our bodies as a living sacrifice, holy and acceptable unto God. With our eyes, our mouths, our hands, our feet, and with our whole being we are to give God praise, honor and glory. We are not our own. We were bought with a price- the crucifixion of Christ! This is our spiritual act- our reasonable act- of worship. We should do this out of gratitude and love that our sins have been forgiven.

When we think about all that God has done for us, He's done too much for us not to worship Him! Therefore, we should pray to God to use our eyes that we might see with eyes of love and compassion; to use our ears that we might hear Him and listen to those in need of empathy and understanding; that we might use our mouths that through Christ we will speak words of life, kindness and encouragement; and that we might be a witness of Christ to the world. Pray that we use our hands and our feet that we might minister to others, lift up and exalt the name of Jesus, and bring God's gift of salvation to the lost.

Following God's commandments involve action. It involves work. It is not simply listening to what God says. We must actively do what the Lord commands. Jesus gave Himself as the ultimate and pure sacrifice for our sins. Therefore, we must ask ourselves, what are we willing to sacrifice, what are we willing to do, what are we willing to give for Him?

Time for reflection! Pray for a moment. Ask God to reveal these answers to you.

What thoughts, attitudes, actions, behaviors, or lifestyle habits hinder you from daily committing your bodies and resources to God for His use? Acknowledge them and list those here:

_____

_____

_____

_____

_____

_____

What sacrifices could you make or priorities could you change to provide the time and resources for you to do God's work? How can you demonstrate your faith to willingly allow God to handle your challenges? Journal your answers below.

_____

_____

_____

_____

_____

_____

_____

_____

_____

Did you write them down? It is impossible to address what you fail to acknowledge. Similar to an alcoholic, he or she cannot confront and reconcile the problem of being an alcoholic if they never admit and accept the fact that they have a problem; they are an alcoholic. You cannot address and resolve whatever issue(s) hinder you from committing your bodies and resources to God if you never acknowledge what habits, behaviors, attitudes or lifestyle habits prevent you from doing so.

Share this information with an accountability partner. Having someone you trust to help you face your challenges, through the love of Christ, helps you to overcome your barriers. Pray for God's strength to conquer your weaknesses.

Day 17

Being Doers of God's Word

~~~

"But be doers of the word, and not hearers only, deceiving your selves.
For if anyone is a hearer of the word and not a doer, he is like a man
observing his natural face in a mirror." (James 1:22, 23 NKJV)

Scripture commands that we become practitioners of God's Word, not just hearers.

The Bible clearly states "do not merely listen to the Word, and so deceive yourselves. Do what it says. Anyone who listens to the Word but does not do what it says is like a man who looks at his face in a mirror and, after looking at himself, goes away and immediately forgets what he looks like".[1] In other words, you forget who you are, whose you are, and what you've been called to do. As worshippers of

Christ, we are to be about our Father's business and to follow His commandments.

We are to actively pursue what Christ desires. We must stop looking for and offering excuses to not follow God's instructions. Do what He says. When directed to confront Pharaoh to release the Israelites from captivity, Moses first offered excuses- his lack of eloquence and his slowness of speech- to not do what God desired (read Exodus 4: 10-17). The Lord became angry with Moses. Like Moses, our sinful nature wants to keep us from doing God's Will and God's work. Being doers of God's Word involves committing our whole self to Him. It involves maximizing and using the provisions God has already provided for us to accomplish His handiwork. Specifically, if God has chosen you for a particular mission, He will also provide the means to successfully accomplish the task, as He did for Moses. You just have to do it!

We must be obedient to God. Our greatest challenge is to be submissive; to surrender to His Will and not our own. Our responsibility is to become a witness of Christ to the world- to represent and re-present Christ to others; to continue the spread of the gospel and to declare the truth without compromise. Our duty is to do God's bidding despite the cost. Ours is to live life as a living sacrifice, pouring out the love of God to others in service and ministry for the sake of Christ.

Our charge is to keep the faith; to continue to serve Christ and to abound and flourish in the work of the Lord, whatever He has called us to do. We must never grow weary of working for Christ. Paul reminds us in the first book of Corinthians, "therefore, my beloved brethren, be ye stedfast, unmovable, always abounding in the work of the Lord, forasmuch as ye know that your labour is not in vain in the Lord."[2] Therefore, we must intentionally live out the Word of God daily. This might be rather challenging if we lean only on our own strength and ability to persevere. Thus, it is extremely important that we integrate all of our being, all of our strength and resilience, and our will and determination under the lordship of Christ.

To be successful in our quest, we must continually abide in Him and stay connected to the source of our strength- the Lord Jesus Christ. Jesus adamantly teaches us that- "I am the vine, ye are the branches: He that abideth [or remains] in me, and I in him, the same bringeth forth much fruit; for without me, ye [you] can do nothing."[3] Commentators in the Life Application Bible further clarify abiding or "remaining in Christ" as: "(1) believing that He is God's Son (I John 4:15),

(2) receiving Him as [your] Savior and Lord (John 1:12), (3) doing what God says (I John 3:24), (4) continuing to believe the gospel (1John 2:24), and (5) relating in love to the community of believers- Christ's body (John 15:12)."[4]

The result of not staying and growing in Christ is death- the death of your fruitfulness and your special relationship with Christ. The Bible says- "If anyone does not remain in [Christ], he is like a branch that is thrown away and withers; such branches are picked up, thrown into the fire and burned."[5] As with any kind of vine, the branches that grow from the main trunk cannot sustain life unless it stays connected to the core vine. If it is broken off or separated, that branch will soon wither and die. No leaves, no fruit- nothing- will grow, and it soon decays. It is then good for nothing, and is gathered as waste and burned.

The same is true of our lives and the fruit of our lives. Jesus is The Vine. We are the branches. If we do not stay connected to Him by following His commandments and doing His Will, nothing (or "no- thing", as one of my friends would always say) we attempt to do will prosper and will soon perish. But, if we remain in Christ by staying connected to Him, continually growing in the knowledge and truth of Christ, and working to do the Will of God, then we shall produce much fruit for our Father. We will be successful in leading other souls to Christ and obtaining great results in our work despite the challenges and road blocks that face us in our daily lives. Those who choose not to bear fruit for God or who try to block the efforts of God's saints, will be cut off from His life-giving power.

The Bible instructs us to "be filled with the Spirit."[6] Therefore, ask the Holy Spirit to fill you, to guide you, to teach and strengthen you that you may fulfill the work Christ has called you to do. Pray that you learn to not fight against the Will of God. Pray that you learn to be obedient and submissive to God's Will and to God's way. Pray for your ability to stay closely connected to Christ, to do what He says, to finish the course, persevering in godliness so that you may remain qualified to perform effective ministry (1 Corinthians 9:27). Pray to become doers of God's Word; to actively use the spiritual gifts and take advantage of the other provisions that God has provided you. In doing so, you will grow from simply being a hearer of God's Word to being a servant of God. This is yet another facet of worship.

Our hope and our prayer should be that when we come to the end of our lives, like the Apostle Paul, we will have lived as doers of the Word of God- "having fought the good fight, having kept the faith, and having finished the race and the work that He has called us to do" (2 Timothy 4:7).[7] This is our mandate, and this should be our petition to Christ.

Have you looked in the mirror lately? Did you see a reflection of Christ? Did you see yourself as His servant? Are you willing to do His bidding, complete His handiwork and be committed to His cause? Pray with me as we ask God to help us in this area.

Father, teach us and help us to become doers of Your word. Grant, dear Father, that we persevere in the work that You have given us to do. Let us not grow faint or weary. Provide us the strength, the ability, the resourcefulness, the longsuffering, and commitment needed to remain qualified to maintain an effective ministry. Help us fulfill the work you have called us to do. Thank you God for choosing us to be your vessels- your workers here on earth. Use us, Father, according to your will. It is in the precious name of Jesus I pray. Amen.

Examination time! Meditate on these questions, and pray on your answers before responding.

1) What excuses do you often present to the Lord to avoid doing His work?

_____

_____

_____

_____

2) What impedes you from performing effective ministry and leading others to Christ?

_____

_____

_____

_____

3) Are you bearing any visible fruit for God? What fruit would others say they see in you?

_____

_____

_____

_____

4) Pinpoint how you can become a doer of God's Word by unselfishly putting your resources and your energy to work for Christ?

_____

_____

_____

_____

_____

_____

_____

_____

Prayer Reflection

What has God spoken to you in your prayers?

_____

_____

_____

_____

_____

_____

_____

_____

What did you say or promise God?

_____

_____

_____

_____

_____

_____

_____

_____

Day 18

Being Committed

~~~

"That good thing which was committed unto thee keep by the Holy

Ghost which dwelleth in us."

(2 Timothy1:14, KJV)

J esus is looking for committed followers.

Prayerfully, I hope you've asked God to help you identify what He has called you to do in kingdom building. You've identified your gifts. Now, God wants you to boldly maximize and utilize the gifts that the Holy Spirit has entrusted in you.

God wants you to be fully committed in doing His work. Jesus was sincerely committed to God's purpose which made His ministry on this earth highly effective. Our development

179

in every aspect of our Christian life and personal ministry directly depends on our commitment to God's purpose.

In fact, Jesus tells us "if any man will come after me, let him deny himself, and take up his cross daily, and follow me."[1] Being committed, then, is a full-time job; not just a part-time assignment. It involves the total surrender of self and the perpetual development of a Godly character. Christ's way of life becomes your way of life. His values become your values. It is a call to walk differently from the world; a call to live differently from the flow of society. It is more than just merely being involved in God's work; it is making God's work part of your lifestyle. It is more than shifting a few priorities; it is giving Christ preeminence and making the work of Christ our number one priority. It is more than temporarily redirecting our focus from our personal concerns; it is making the work of Christ our permanent focus. It is a call to be committed to His Will, His Word and His Work. It is a call to a singleness of heart, mind, and soul; a call to reflect God, to live pure, to walk in integrity, to follow the commandments of Christ and to lead others to salvation. Will you make a commitment to God to willingly give of your time, energy and resources to continue the work of Christ? Will you make a commitment to a cause greater than yourself?

Making the Commitment

This would be an excellent time to read the New Testament book of Second Timothy. Here the Apostle Paul gives helpful advice to young Timothy to remain solidly grounded in Christian service, to stay steadfast, and to endure the sacrifices and sufferings ahead. As with many of us, Timothy would find it is easy to want to quit during difficult times.

We must have a strong foundation in the Lord in order to stay committed to His service. The Holy Spirit helps us to remain strong and loyal, even in the face of our fears, challenges, struggles, heartbreaks and disappointments. To survive and succeed despite a sundry of road blocks, we must take our eyes off of the people and things that tend to discourage us. We must keep our eyes firmly fixed on Christ, for He is the source of our help and strength.

Stop worrying about what people think or how they might respond. Look only to God. Never underestimate the strength and courage that resides in you through Christ.

Even doing what we might think are simple things can become an onerous undertaking if we allow the devil and negative people around us to "get inside our heads". However, both Apostles Matthew and Mark assure us that despite our fears and misgivings, "with God all things are possible" (Matthew 19:26; Mark 10:27). We must believe and know with total confidence that God will supply all of our needs. He will equip us for whatever task He has assigned us to do. That doesn't mean it will be easy or that you won't have some challenges and hard times ahead of you. But if you persevere, and maintain faith in God, you will succeed.

We often read the various accounts of the people in the Bible and think – "but they were a special people. They had a special ability to remain committed to God and to do what He asked of them". True. The people used by God were special to Him. But you are also special to God. God used ordinary people-just like you- to do extraordinary things then, and He uses ordinary people to do extraordinary things even now. God has not changed! God himself confirms in the book of Malachi that: "... I am the Lord, I change not." [2] God has not stopped giving special abilities to meet the tasks He has given us to do.

We all have a job to do. We each have a special task. And it is certain that God will equip us for whatever He has assigned us to do. Our charge is to be committed, to be faithful, and to complete the mission- whatever our role.

One very simple evangelistic task we all have as believers -which we so often take for granted and do half-heartedly- is welcoming people into the house of the Lord. Our duty- whether you're an usher or just a blood-cleansed member of the congregation- is to help people feel comfortable, and to feel accepted; to feel love as they enter into God's house. Our mission is to acknowledge them, to make them feel wanted; to make them feel it is our honest desire that they come, and then come back to learn of the love of Christ. It might seem a small task, but it is very important. Why? Because people will not repeatedly return to where they don't feel welcomed; and they won't return to hear the Word of God if they don't feel welcomed by the professed people of God. Therefore, allowing God to use us in helping people feel accepted, at ease and embraced; to feel that they matter as they enter, become engulfed in worship, and leave God's house is just a small part in letting them know God loves them. It is part of our reasonable service. It is part of *your* reasonable service. A simple smile and acknowledgement, a genuine welcome and polite handshake; an innocent touch or a Christian hug can do wonders in opening hearts to be receptive to God. It is an inelaborate task, but one to which we should all be committed. Thus, by helping to create a loving and inviting atmosphere where people will want to come to hear the Word of God, those who are unsaved might eventually give their lives to Christ.

Beware, there may be times when the people we serve may not be very receptive, grateful or even appreciative of what we do-whether it's great or small- but persevere. Put emphasis on the act of serving in love, and the ultimate recipient of our service- God. We must remember that many of the people coming into God's sanctuary and ultimately coming to God are hurting and lost. They don't yet know how to appreciate the goodness of God. They may not appreciate you. They just feel their pain and sense of emptiness. Love them anyway. Be respectful towards them anyway. Do as God has commanded you to do, in spite of their apparent rejection. Jesus was rejected. Remember, it is for God that we work- not man. It is to God that we are to be committed.

A Cause Greater than Yourself

Many people today shy away from making commitments, but I ask again, will you make a commitment to Christ? Will you make a commitment to use your gifts, talents and time for kingdom building; a commitment to a cause greater than yourself?

Unfortunately, this is one of the greatest problems in the church today. People want to spectate but not make a commitment. They want to assemble in worship service on the Sabbath, but not work for Christ during the week.

You might ask: "So what will my commitment involve? What am I being asked to give up? What are you actually asking me to do?" I'm glad you asked. In fact, most people experience fear over those very questions; many will balk at those exact concerns. But fear discounts your faith. You must learn to control and quiet your fears with the Word of God.

You might also be asking –"How much time is going to be required? Thinking, "I have a busy schedule. I really don't have the time. I work two jobs; or I have kids at home and they have numerous activities". Or you might have thoughts like: "I don't like to get up in front of people. I'm not comfortable talking to strangers. I get nervous. I am struggling with this 'Christian-thing' myself, so what exactly are you asking of me?"

Being committed is the act of intentionally not being complacent; daring to live for Christ; to use your time, talents and spiritual gifts for the enriching of His kingdom. It requires the objective and decisive yielding or surrendering of your will to do the Will of God. It may mean making some personal sacrifices of your time and resources for the benefit of God and His people. But God's not asking you to give away your life's savings. Nor is He asking you to neglect your family or other important responsibilities, or to do those things which you are not capable of doing. He *is* asking that you surrender yourself to become a chosen vessel to be used for His purpose; to get up off that pew (and off that couch) and get to work for Christ- even on those days you don't necessarily feel like it. Remember, it's not about how you feel; it's about *doing* God's Will.

Being committed means making a conscious decision sometimes to not take the easy road and do what you want to do or what you feel like doing, but to submissively obey and do what God would have you to do. It is the process and unswerving response of denying yourself, daily, and taking up the cause and cross of Christ. It means being fully dedicated and invested in the work of salvation. But, this commitment must be made with an open and willing heart.

With our time, talents, and spiritual gifts, as with our money, God wants us to be a cheerful giver. As the Apostle Paul reminds us in his letter to the church at Corinth, "each man should give what he has decided in his heart to give, not reluctantly or under compulsion, for God loves a cheerful giver" (2 Cor. 9:7).[3] If we do anything for Christ that we really don't want to do, we may as well *not* do it. God knows our hearts. He knows our minds. He knows our motives. And God doesn't want coerced or constrained service. That is a false sacrifice. That is false commitment.

God may not be calling you to be a missionary, a preacher, a Sunday-School teacher or anything of that magnitude. That certainly takes a special gift and a special calling. But each and every child of God has an irrevocable calling to carry on the work of Christ. Each of us has been called to make a difference. How you serve will look different based on your calling. However, God will not ask you to do anything He has not already equipped you to handle. Whatever your gift, whatever the amount of time you have available, commit it to the cause of Christ.

Examine yourself. Meditate on these questions and then journal your answers below. Then, if you are ready to be committed to the work of Christ, sign the commitment statement.

What draws you away from being fully committed to Christ?

_____

_____

_____

_____

What do you fear losing if you commit your life to Christ (i.e. friends, personal dreams, time, possessions)?

_____

_____

_____

_____

What might you gain by committing your life to Christ?

_____

_____

_____

_____

My Commitment to Christ

Father, I commit myself to You for Your purpose. Use my talents, skills, abilities, and spiritual gifts as You see fit in the uplift and building of Your kingdom. Lord, I willingly make myself available to You. Use me as Your chosen vessel. Search my heart that my motives are pure so that You may be exalted. Help me face my fears and fill my mind with Your Word that I may receive Your strength. Reveal to me Father, where You want me to work and what You want me to do. Help me to make a difference in my generation. May all glory and honor belong to You. In Jesus' name I pray and commit to you this day. Amen.

_____

Name

_____

Date

Day 19

Called to Make a Difference

∿

"And the Lord came, and stood, and called as at other times,

Samuel, Samuel. Then Samuel answered, Speak; for thy

servant heareth" (1 Samuel 3:8, KJV)

We have all been called to make a difference in our generation.

God has a special task just for you. Maybe it's helping with Vacation Bible School- if not teaching, maybe assisting with the crafts or music. Maybe it's working as a hallway or classroom monitor, or providing needed security. Perhaps it's assisting in the nursery, children's church, the youth ministry or some other ministry within your local church to help bring unrepentant souls into the vineyard of Christ. Conceivably you could be a mentor, or maybe it's sharing your specific story with others that have experienced some of the same challenges you've already faced and overcome. Perhaps your gifts have been targeted to be used outside the walls of your local church in missions or other outreach. There is much work to be done in the prisons, community shelters and other places where the Word needs to be carried and the work of God needs to be done. The opportunities are inexhaustible. God is not asking you to do everything, but He is asking you to do something. He is calling you to make a difference!

Your assigned task may involve just a few hours a week, or a few hours a month. It may be assisting someone behind the scenes, or it may cast you in the spotlight. Remember, each of us has been given a different gift to be used for different and special tasks. Some of us can do one task well; others may be better equipped to do another. We need to pray and ask God how our talents and gifts uniquely fit into His plan for the benefit of His body- the people of God. And all of His people may not yet be within the church. We must go to them, search for them, and reach them wherever they are.

God uses those who willingly make themselves available to Him. We have the responsibility to help others grow and develop in their Christian lives; to help them become disciples, and then to become better disciples. Remember the directive given by Christ in the Great Commission to "therefore go and make disciples of all nations, ...and teaching them to obey everything I have commanded you..." (Matthew 28: 19-20 NIV)?[1]

God is not asking you to do this alone. If we obey the direction of God as we work with others, together we can accomplish more than any of us could do alone. It is a human tendency to underestimate what we can do as a group. But as a unified body in Christ, we can accomplish more together than we could ever dream possible doing by ourselves. Working together, the church can express the fullness of Christ.

Fill your mind with Scripture and gain confidence in what God can do through you. Don't focus on what you can or cannot do alone. Pray and ask God to reveal to you where He wants you to work and what He wants you to do. Then do it!

Dare to live, work and perform beyond your self-imposed or external-imposed limits. Dare to defy the naysayers and to push past your excuses. Dare to just begin; don't wait to be perfect- or you'll never get started. Dare to look pass the size of the task, and say "I can't". Rather, behold the magnificence of our God and know that He can! Be as the writer of Psalm 121 who exclaimed-"I will lift up mine eyes unto the hills, from whence cometh my help. My help cometh from the Lord which made heaven and earth."[2] The anonymous writer of this Psalm goes further to testify that God "will not let your foot slip...the Lord watches over you...[and] will keep you from all harm-He will watch over your life; [He] will watch over your coming and going both now and forevermore."[3] We must have faith and trust in God's Word. His Word does not lie. Know that through Christ, you can do more than you ever dreamed or imaged. In fact, in the Gospel according to Mark, Jesus said-"If you can believe, all things are possible to him who believes."[4] Sincere and unmovable faith in God is all you need to handle any undertaking. Sincere and unmovable faith is not just saying that we can trust God, but that God can trust us to accomplish what He has set before us.

We must be bold in the Lord, and be committed to do whatever He puts before us if we are to make a difference in this world. God promises to give us strength to meet our challenges. He doesn't promise to eliminate or completely remove them, for if we had no rough roads to walk, no mountains to climb, or no battles to fight, we would never grow.

God does not leave us alone in our challenges. He stands beside us, teaches us and strengthens us to face whatever challenge that comes before us. To stand strong in the Lord, internalize the following guidelines:

Crush discouragement! Don't just try to avoid it. Crush it! Conquer it! Obliterate it! We all get discouraged from time to time. But, we can't waddle in self-pity parties or emulate Chicken Little- always thinking the sky is falling. Surround yourself with positive, God-fearing people who will help you accomplish your task, share a word of encouragement from the Lord, and give you the support you need.

Trust God! Don't rely on yourself. Trust God to give you everything you need to get the job done. Remember, the devil doesn't want you to do anything. He doesn't want you to succeed! He wants to keep you discouraged, distracted, and dismayed. He doesn't want the work of the Lord to be completed. He knows that when it is, he is doomed and defeated. Christ has already guaranteed our victory! You may even fail in your tasks from time to time, but don't stop; don't give up! Learn from your failures. Get up! Brush yourself off! Analyze the setbacks, and begin again. Glean determination from your disappointments! Don't let anything take your eyes off of your goal and your commitment to Christ.

Fight to be effective! We must put aside everything that will daunt and dishearten us from being effective Christians and doing the work of the Lord. As the Hebrew Christians were warned: "...lay aside every weight, and the sin which doth so easily beset us, and let us run with patience the race that is set before us...."[5] Or as translated in the New International Version- "... let us throw off everything that hinders and the sin that so easily entangles, and let us run with perseverance the race marked out for us."[6] Repeat as often as we must – "God did not give us a spirit of fear, but of power, and of love, and of a sound mind" (2 Timothy 1:6).[7]

So, what is holding you back? Fear? Lack of confidence? Awaiting validation by man? Not wanting to separate yourself from the crowd? Loss of friends? Peer pressure? What?

We must continue pressing toward the goal as we are reminded by the Apostle Paul (Philippians 3:14) where he proclaims- "I press on toward the goal to win the prize for which God has called me heavenward in Christ Jesus"[8]

My challenge to you is to get up off those pews! Stop procrastinating! Stop looking for excuses! There is work to be done! Scripture tells us "the harvest is plentiful, but the workers are few."[9] You were called to make a difference.

Christ is looking for great worshippers. God is looking for single-hearted servants willing to work for Him. Make a commitment to work, to give back to God for all He has done for you. Make a commitment to Christ and get up off those pews!

Time for reflection! Have you taken the time to ask God what He has called you to do? If not, pause and do so right now. As before, meditate on these questions and then journal your answers below.

1) What do *you* think God desires that you do?

_____

_____

_____

_____

_____

2) What services are needed in your church that are not being met that you have the capacity to do? In your community?

_____

_____

_____

_____

_____

3) What is God placing on your heart that you keep ignoring and turning your back on?

_____

_____

_____

_____

_____

4) What difference can you make in the lives of those around you to help lead them to Christ?

_____

_____

_____

_____

_____

_____

Day 20

Mirroring Great Worshippers

~~~

"Give unto the Lord the glory due unto His name;

bring an offering, and come before Him: worship the Lord

in the beauty of holiness."(1 Chronicles 16:29)

W e are to give God the glory due to His name.
Are you still wondering what God is looking for
in a true worshipper? What He wants from us? What He
wants from you? We should take our cues on how to be the
worshipper that God seeks from the mighty models found
in the Bible. Read their accounts. There are several both in
the Old and the New Testament- mighty men and women of
God. I will only highlight a few. The many not listed here are
every bit as important and certainly as impactful as the small
number I include.

I'm going to ask you to do a lot more soul searching and reflection on this day of our journey. We're almost done, but here our expedition gets a little more rigorous. Your spiritual muscles should be sufficiently warm by now to handle extra introspection. Thus, today's examination is constructed a little differently. Indeed, it is much longer, but you can handle it! So, review, evaluate, and digest the examples of these great worshippers; really think about how we too should relate to and worship Christ.

Great Worshippers

Job was a great worshipper. If you don't know his story, read the book of Job in the Old Testament. In spite of his trials and tribulations, the lost of his wealth, his family, and his health, in good times and in bad, he continued to worship the Lord and give God praise.

We too must learn to worship God in spite of what is happening around us. We can't be "fair-weather worshippers" only - worshipping God only when things are going well for us and for the prosperity He provides. We must trust God in all His ways and cleave unto His understanding. We must repent of our doubts, fears and failings. It is not enough for us to recognize the great truths of God; we must live out

God's truths each and every day. No matter what the situation, we must put our faith into practice. That can sometimes be very difficult. Our greatest test is to trust God's goodness even when we don't understand His goal. This may not be easy. But we must learn to acknowledge and confess God's lordship although everything around us is in shambles- like Job. We must love and praise God regardless of whether He allows blessings or suffering to come to us. All has its purpose in continuously molding us into the image of Christ.

A challenge? Yes! Testing can be difficult. It was difficult even for Job. But the result is often a deeper and stronger relationship with God. The true worshipper must learn to proclaim "the Lord gave, and the Lord hath taken away; blessed be the name of the Lord!"[1] –although everything around us is crashing and our hearts are crushed. God can heal broken hearts. God can strengthen us even when all of our strength is depleted! We must keep our eyes on Christ- not on the crisis! There will be times we will hurt, and times when we will feel some loss or despair. We may desire to question God or even get angry. But as Moses spoke to the Israelites-"Fear not: for God is come to prove [test] you, and that His fear may be before your faces, that ye sin not."[2] Therefore, in spite of what's happening around us, we must not sin. Like Job, we must develop a "never-the-less" attitude – though trials and tribulations engulf us, we will praise our God never-the-less, and give Him the glory due to His name. If we keep our hands in God's hand and trust God to deliver us, comfort and joy will come. It is in those times, we must truly rely on a strong and deeply-rooted faith in God. We must be like the tree firmly planted by the rivers of water. As the author of Psalm1 writes: "He is like a tree planted by the streams of water, which yields its fruit in season and whose leaf does not wither. Whatever he does prospers" (Psalm 1:3).[3] The more we trust in God's Word and believe in God's promises, the more fruitful we will be. As a tree requires ample water to bear luscious fruit, we must be rooted in God's Word in order to produce actions and attitudes that honor and lift up the name of our Savior. We must know that in the end, through Christ, we will prevail and be triumphant. As Job, we must learn that in all things, in all situations, we must give God praise and continue to worship Him for who He is.

Carrots, Eggs and Coffee Beans

I'm sure you've read many different allegories of how people respond to testing. One of my favorites, that has traveled the internet numerous times with questions regarding the actual author, describes how things respond differently to boiling water. The tale goes like this:

A young woman went to her mother and told her how terribly difficult things were for her. She didn't know how she was going to make it and wanted to give up. It seemed as one problem was resolved, a new problem would surface.

Her mother took her to the kitchen. Quietly, the mother filled three pots with water and placed each on the stove. Soon the water in each of the pots came to a boil. In the first pot the mother placed carrots, in the second she placed eggs, and in the third she placed ground coffee beans. She let them sit and boil without saying a word.

After twenty minutes she turned off the burners. She fished the carrots out of the first pot and placed them in a bowl. She lifted the eggs out of the second pot and also placed them in a bowl. She then ladled the coffee out of its pot and placed it in a cup.

Turning to her daughter, she asked, "Tell me what you see." "Carrots, eggs, and coffee," the daughter replied.

Her mother brought her closer and asked her to feel the carrots. The daughter did and noted that they were warm and soft. The mother then asked her to take an egg and break it. After removing the shell, the daughter observed the eggs were solid and hard-boiled. Finally, the mother asked her to sip the coffee.

"Hmmmm!" The daughter smiled, as she sampled its rich, savory taste. The daughter then asked, "What was the significance of each food item? What are you trying to say?"

Her mother explained that each of these objects had faced the same adversity: boiling water. Each reacted differently. The carrots went in strong, hard, and unrelenting. After being subjected to the boiling water, they softened and became weak. The eggs had been fragile. The thin outer shell had protected the gelatinous interior, but after sitting through the boiling water, the insides became firm and hardened. The ground coffee beans were unique, however. After they were in the boiling water, they changed the water!

"Which are you?" she asked her daughter. "When adversity knocks on your door how do you respond? Are you a carrot, an egg or a coffee bean?"

Examine yourself. How do you respond to God's testing? Are you the carrot that seems strong, but with pain and adversity you wilt, become soft and lose your strength? Are you the egg that starts with a pliable heart, but hardens with the heat and strain of life? Did you begin with a fluid, supple spirit, but after the death of a loved one, an ugly disagreement within the church, a financial hardship or some other trial, you became callused and rigid? Has your external shell remained intact, but your soul has become bitter and harsh with an unpleasant spirit, and a hard-edged and hurting heart? Or are you like the coffee bean? The ground beans actually changed the hot water- the very circumstance that caused the pain.

When the water began to boil, it released the true nature of the coffee bean, its enticing aroma and its rich, welcoming flavor. If you are like the coffee beans, when things are at their worst, you've found you can rely on God and He can change the situation around you. You become the victor, not the victim.

How about you? How do you handle adversity? Are you a carrot, an egg or a coffee bean? Give examples to validate your answer. Pray that God will give you the strength, courage and perseverance to handle any adversity that comes your way.

_____

_____

_____

_____

_____

_____

_____

_____

_____

Back to our model worshippers, David was another great worshipper. Read his account beginning in First Chronicles, Chapter Ten. Few men or women in the Bible were as close to God as David. David had frequent communication with God which increased his capacity to worship, and strengthened his desire to be obedient. Yet, David sinned. David was not perfect. We should strive to worship after the spirit-led ways of David.

☐ **David recognized that only God was worthy of total devotion.** We must also recognize that God and God alone is worthy of our devotion, praise, and worship. As David was an example for his people, we must also be an example for others to follow. We must help others recognize that only God is worthy of all praise, of all honor, and of all glory. We are not to put the importance of anything before God.

☐ **David was humble before the Lord that God might be exalted.** Although David was king over all Israel, David was humble before Almighty God. While David accumulated much wealth, he dedicated that wealth to God for His service (1 Chron. 18:11). David realized that all of his wealth and blessings came from God. We too must remember that status and material things have no lasting value. We must always remain humble before God and not think of ourselves "more highly than we ought" (Romans 12:3).[4] It is dangerously easy to think our financial and material blessings are the result of our own labor, but we must remember that "every good and perfect gift is from above..."[5] We must not allow possessions or man's opinion of us to distort our own importance. Even small successes and spotlights of attention can often cause us to become arrogant and proud. Be careful! All honor and all praise is to be directed to God. We must be watchful that we don't get "puffed up", and that we remain humble so that the Lord can be exalted.

☐ **David continually sought God's Will and direction. And God answered.** David was successful because of his consistent trust in God. David would ask God for His direction and His presence. When David failed to do so, he would repent and ask the Lord for direction and guidance before moving forward. Far too often, we wait until we are in trouble before we turn to God. We turn to God as our *last* resort instead of our first. We get in a hurry and fail to wait for God to answer us. God should always be our first source of help, *not* our last. The Bible tells us "now devote your heart and your soul to seeking the Lord your God."[6] As worshippers, we must consistently ask God for His direction and then follow His guidance. Seeking God must become a part of our lifestyles. We must also diligently teach our children to seek God and honor His commandments and His ways as an inheritance to them. Nothing we leave to our children provides as much value as the spiritual guidance we impart. We must become a "David" and continually inquire of God regarding His Will and His direction for our lives. We must seek Him first. Then, we must pray and wait for Him to answer.

☐ **David was repentant and learned from his mistakes.** David sinned. Yet, above everything else, David worshipped God. He had an unwavering belief in the faithful and forgiving nature of God, and stretched out his heart in genuine repentance (1 Chron. 21:8, 17). We must be as David when we sin. It is not enough to simply repent and correct what is wrong. We must actively pursue what is right. Although God is a forgiving God, we must not take His forgiveness lightly nor His blessings for granted. We must be careful to seek and keep all of God's commandments and to be prepared to understand and accept the consequences when we fail to do so. When David failed to follow God's direction when first attempting to take the Ark of the Covenant to Jerusalem, Uzzah paid with his life (1 Chron. 13:5-13). Upon David's second attempt, however, he asked for and followed God's directions, and was then successful in his pursuit (1 Chron. 15:13-15).

We too must learn from our mistakes. We must consistently ask God for His direction and then abide by His teachings. We must worship God, and always be ready to earnestly repent of our sins and turn to God for forgiveness.

☐ **David eagerly expressed his thanks to God.** David noted in his Psalm of Thanksgiving that we should:

"Give thanks to the Lord, call on His name; make known among the nations what He has done. Sing to Him, sing praise to Him; tell of all His wonderful acts. Glory in His holy name; let the hearts of those who seek the Lord rejoice. Look to the Lord and His strength; seek His face always. Remember the wonders He has done, His miracles, and the judgments He pronounced..."[7]

As noted in David's psalm, our response of thanksgiving should include: (1) calling on His name, (2) telling others specifically what God has done for us, (3) glorifying His name and rejoicing in Him (4) seeking His face always, and

(5) remembering the wonders, miracles and judgments He has done; remembering His mercy and His grace; remembering His patience and His longsuffering. Praise and thanksgiving should be a regular part of every worshipper's lifestyle. We should praise God continually. We should manifest our praise by offering ourselves, our time and our resources in tribute and worship to Christ. We should eagerly and earnestly declare God's character and His attributes. We should recognize and affirm His goodness. We should ascribe to God the glory and honor that is due to His name.

While there is much we can learn from David, let's consider a few more mighty followers of God. Let's examine what they can teach us about being devoted worshippers.

As stated earlier, many great believers are chronicled throughout the Old and New Testament. We all know of Mary, the mother of Jesus- one who witnessed both His birth and His death; who honored Him as her son and her Savior- a true worshipper. We know of the work and worship of the disciples who followed Christ. But, let's look at one we least think about, and one of whom we should give more thought and comparison regarding how to usher up authentic worship.

Mary of Bethany, the sister of Martha and Lazarus is a great example. Mary and Martha both loved Jesus deeply and served Him during His visits to their home. But Martha's desire to serve Him actually resulted in her spending little valuable time with Christ. While the act of hospitality was very important in their culture and time, nothing should take the place of spending quality time with the Lord. Martha's time and efforts were spent in making preparations and seeing that Christ was comfortable- important, but busy work –"hosting chores". She failed to bask in His presence; to make Christ preeminent in her life.

Mary, instead, chose to spend time at the feet of Jesus. Mary put dwelling in the presence of Jesus as her priority rather than being involved with the more superficial and mundane requirements of life (Luke 10:39-41). Mary realized that being in the presence of God took ultimate priority. In the presence of Christ, she found joy, strength, fulfillment and spiritual peace. As the Passover approached, and as Lazarus, the disciples and others sat with Jesus, Mary approached Christ and poured precious ointment on His head and wiped His feet with her hair to show her complete love, devotion and unselfish act of worship to Him (Matthew 26:6-13; Mark 14: 3-9; John 12:1-8). The disciples ridiculed her and thought the expensive oil could have been better used for other purposes.

While both Martha and the disciples complained about Mary's actions and behavior in two separate incidents, Christ commended her for her unselfish act of genuine love and devotion. Christ praised Mary for her desire to spend indispensable time with Him, and to give of herself and her most precious gifts to honor Him, to learn from Him, to bask in His presence and His glory.

Luke records Jesus saying: "but one thing is needed, and Mary has chosen that good part, which will not be taken away from her".[8] Mary worshipped as Christ desired. In this same way, we should also desire to sit at the feet of Jesus, and take time to relish in His presence. We should make Christ our priority and to delight in His glory.

The very essence of worshipping Christ is to regard Him in the highest esteem- with the utmost love, respect and devotion; to spend valuable time with Him and to be willing to sacrifice what is most precious to us for His sake and His glory as Mary did.

While our work and service is a very important part of worship, we must be cautious that we don't get caught up in doing "church chores" or taking part in an overabundance of minor activities that we neglect to spend critical time worshipping and being in the presence of Christ. We must ensure our priorities are straight- Christ first, all else second.

We must also be conscientious that our work and service for Christ does not dissolve into mere busywork and self-serving ceremony.

We must guard against working for Christ only because we feel compelled to do so while no longer having any love, passion or desire for what we are doing. We should examine any service that is no longer full of devotion to God. We must examine our motives to ensure our reasons for working are pure. We must be vigilant to not get so caught up in our positions or our projects within the church that we forget the focus of our purpose. We must be diligent in searching our hearts to ensure our motives for doing whatever our tasks are untainted and just; centered and focused on willingly and lovingly doing God's Will and not our own.

Examine yourself. Be incredibly honest. Be truthful with God, even if it's painful. God already knows. Pray that

God searches you and reveals what's in your heart. Psalm 139:23 NIV implores: "Search me, O God, and know my heart; test me and know my anxious thoughts."[9] Record your responses to the following questions and write your answers below:

1) What are your true motives for working for Christ? Are you doing it for the attention and recognition you receive, or are you truly fully committed to Christ and see your work as part of your worship?

_____

_____

_____

_____

_____

2) How would you respond if your name was never acknowledged for the work you rendered? Would you quickly become disgruntled, stop the effort or leave the church?

_____

_____

_____

_____

_____

_____

3) Do you find yourself so busy working in the church that you spend little time worshipping God and expend even less time in His presence?

_____

_____

_____

_____

_____

_____

4) Are you more like Mary or Martha in your efforts to serve God?

_____

_____

_____

_____

_____

_____

5) What will you do to be more like Mary?

_____

_____

_____

_____

_____

_____

_____

6) What will you do to be more like Job and David?

_____

_____

_____

_____

_____

_____

_____

Finally, let's spotlight John the Baptist. Most likely we've all heard of John the Baptist, the cousin of Jesus, but have we closely examined his example of being a great and true worshipper of Christ? Have we stopped to critically analyze how we might emulate John in our worship? Let's study him a little deeper.

☐ **John the Baptist excitedly worshipped Christ.** Even while still in his mother's womb, John leaped with excitement and reverence in the presence of Christ (Luke 1:41, 44). Our worship should also show our excitement and enthusiasm about our risen Savior. Our worship should evoke others' desire to know about our God! We can't draw others to Christ if we never exhibit a life on fire for Him! Non-believers will not be drawn to Christ if we constantly look like we're begrudgingly carrying His cross on our backs. God wants loving, enthusiastic disciples who will demonstrate His love to a dying world, not lukewarm and dispassionate supporters who turn the lost away from Christ. We must emulate John's excitement, his joy and his reverence for Christ as we exalt Him in our worship.

☐ **John prepared the way for Christ**. John was an evangelist- fervently proclaiming the need for repentance and the coming of Christ (Matthew 3:1-2). His worship of Christ was evident in his actions and his lifestyle. We too are to evangelize the lost; to teach of repentance and to emphasize salvation by faith in Christ. This is Christ's mandate (Matthew 28: 18-20). Today, there are still millions of people who do not know Jesus as their personal Savior. It is God's desire that none be lost. Therefore, we are compelled to share the gospel of Christ to the entire world. We need to prepare the way for them to meet Him. We must bear witness of Christ, even as John "bore witness of Him."[10] We must seek the lost, explain their need for salvation, demonstrate Christ's teachings by our conduct, and point the way to Christ. Displaying God's love to the unsaved is a form of worship. But there is still more to do. There are many believers who have started their Christian walk but have gotten misdirected along the way. Many who have sat down on the job and not matured in their faith. As great worshippers, it is our task to encourage our co-laborers, help guide their Christian development, lift them when they seem weak and weary, and point them back to Christ. Our worship of Christ includes the building of His kingdom. Our worship must bear witness and help prepare the way for Christ.

☐ **John baptized as an outward sign of repentance.** Paul shares with us that "John indeed baptized with a baptism of repentance..."[11] While few of us may participate in the baptizing of new souls for Christ, we are accountable for helping others understand their need for repentance, and for leading souls to salvation. As baptized believers our lives must identify with Christ. As Christians, we must exhibit a changed life- turning from and separating ourselves from our old lives of sin and turning to Christ; we must be transformed if we are to be effective in leading others to Him.

John chose not to conform to his present world. He separated himself from the evil and hypocrisy of his time by living apart from the people and exhibiting a different lifestyle (Matthew 3:4-6). His focus was centered on Christ. The Apostle Paul reminds us "... be not conformed to this world: but be ye transformed by the renewing of your mind, that ye may prove what is the good, and acceptable, and perfect will of God" (Romans 12:2 KJV).[12] We too must walk differently from the world. It is okay to be different! We have been sanctified; we have purposely been set apart. The problem is- we want to live as the world dictates. As I once heard one minister ask the congregation, "It's popular in society right now to be saved, but where is the separation?" Unfortunately, too many times, you can't tell the saved from the unsaved. We are too busy trying to act like the world.

Our lifestyles must reflect the Will and values of Christ. The difference in our lifestyles should cause nonbelievers to wonder what's so unique about us, and then provide us the opportunity to talk to them about Christ.

We must advance God's work. In doing so, we honor and glorify God and show visible indication of our worship of Christ. Our lives must depict more than mere words or ritual. Our lives must produce fruit indicative of our repentance. Our "fruit" should be indicative of the character of Christ. This is worship. Non-believers must be able to see a changed life so they might desire to give their lives to Christ.

☐ **John allowed his role to decrease so that Jesus might increase** (John 3:30). It is easy to grow in self-importance in our lives or on the job, or to even grow jealous or envious of another person's ministry or work within the church. But we must remind ourselves that our mission is simply to lead others to Christ. We must guard against over indulgent self-importance- putting our personal agendas, visions, plans and desires ahead of those of God. Remember, it's all about Christ; it is *not* about us. John the Baptist's willingness to decrease in importance that Christ might take preeminence shows an unusual amount of humility. We must always remain humble. Whatever our role in the building of God's kingdom, we must ensure all focus, all efforts point to Christ and His plan for salvation. Self must decrease, so that Christ might be preeminent. It's all about completing what Christ has anointed us to do that others might be saved. It's about ensuring our worship rightly places Christ in the spotlight; that He is given all honor and all praise and that the world comes to know who our Christ is. Can we, like John, put aside our personal agendas and our self-inflated egos in order to remain focused and devoted to Jesus? Are you willing to decrease in personal status so that Christ and His church can increase?

Examination time! Reflect on the characteristics of John the Baptist, and answer the following questions. Journal your responses below.

1) Can people discover your belief in Christ by observing how you live? How might your lifestyle deny any association with Jesus?

_____

_____

_____

_____

_____

2) What can you do to help prepare the way for Christ?

_____

_____

_____

_____

_____

3) How might a position, title, or place of attention cause us to think more highly of ourselves than we should?

_____

_____

_____

4) List three steps we should take to avoid over inflating our egos.

_____

_____

_____

_____

_____

_____

5) It is often said, the dash on a headstone between your date of birth and your date of death represents the life you lived. Would your dash reflect a life lived for Christ? What legacy would you leave?

_____

_____

_____

_____

_____

_____

So, what say you? Are you willing to follow the many examples that Christ has provided that you might become an authentic worshipper of Him? More importantly, are you willing to follow Christ and lead others to Him as well? Christ has done so much for us. Can't we even give back a plausible portion of our lives to Him? After all, that is our reasonable service. That is what we were made to do.

We have a mighty role as worshippers of Christ. We have a great task to do while here on earth. But our work doesn't stop here. Our role is unending. So why do we take our task so lightly?

Day 21

Infinite Worship

~~~

"And all the angels stood round about the throne, and about the elders

and the four beasts, and fell before the throne on their faces, and

worshipped God, saying, Amen: Blessing, and glory and wisdom, and

thanksgiving, and honour, and power, and might, be unto

our God for ever and ever. Amen."

(Revelation 7:11-12 KJV)

We were made to worship God forever.

By now, I hope we're in unity of agreement that we were made to worship. All the angels in heaven were made to worship God, so how could we possibly think we were made to do anything else? After all, God made us just a little lower than the angels (Psalm 8:5). We too were made to praise and worship Him forever. But our worship doesn't just start in the afterlife. Our worship begins now! Psalm 146:2 states: "I will praise the Lord all my life; I will sing praise to my God as long as I live."[1] In fact, David tells us in Psalm 145:2 –"Every day I will bless You, and I will praise Your name forever and ever." [2] We must take David's lead. Therefore, we are not to wait until we die to begin praising and worshipping the Lord continuously. We are to endlessly worship Him even now.

Ceaseless, infinite worship doesn't stop with us. We must also teach our children and our grandchildren to love and worship our God. David extols in his 145th Psalm of Praise that:

"One generation shall praise Your works to another, and shall declare Your mighty acts. I will meditate on the glorious splendor of Your majesty, and on Your wondrous works. Men shall speak of the might of Your awesome acts, and I will declare Your greatness. They shall utter the memory of Your great goodness, and shall sing of Your righteousness" *(verses 4-7).* *"All Your works shall praise You, O Lord, and Your saints shall bless You. They shall speak of the glory of Your kingdom, and talk of Your power, to make known to the*

sons of men His mighty acts, and the glorious majesty of His
kingdom" (verses 10-12).[3]

Further in this Psalm, David again reminds us to "let all flesh bless His holy name for ever and ever".[4] Thus, our task of providing infinite worship, our role of being authentic worshippers begins when we give our lives to Christ and lasts forever. That is a mighty, mighty task! One we all should take very seriously.

We exist to bring honor and glory to God; to worship and exalt Him for who He is. We must take time to praise God, to recognize all of His blessings towards us, and affirm our commitment to do what He has already set forth for us to do-to honor, serve, and worship Him.

It is our task to center our thoughts and actions on Christ and eliminate whatever takes God's rightful place of preeminence in our lives.

It is our task to follow Him with complete devotion. Therefore, we must renew our minds daily by the Word of God, and prepare our hearts to fully and wholly participate in the worship of the God of our salvation.

It is our task to bring unity to the body of Christ and help others mature in their worship of the only true and living God.

We must develop the practice of giving God praise in everything we do and in everything we face. Praise and thanksgiving should be an integral part of our lives; part of our regular routine; part of who we are. We are to praise God continually, even as His angels praise Him forever and forever.

The basis of our praise is declaring God's character and His attributes in the presence of heaven, and in the presence of every one and every thing on earth. When we recognize and affirm His goodness, we are holding up His perfect and just nature for the entire world to see. This is our charge. This is our job as worshippers; our reasonable service.

Certainly on our own we are not worthy to lift up the name of Christ. But Christ is to be honored in each and every conversation, in each and every relationship, in each and every area of our lives. No area is exempt. It is only through His grace and His mercy that we can open our mouths, empty our hearts, and worship Him as He deserves and desires to be worshipped. It is only through God's grace that we even merit the ability to speak His name. But because of His great love, His goodness and compassion, and His great faithfulness towards us, we have been adopted as the children of God and are indebted to proclaim His righteousness. It should be a *privilege* to do so. It is a birthright we *get* to take part in!

We were made to do a specific job. We were made to be worshippers; made to be co-laborers with Christ; made to disciple the lost, to glorify the name of Jesus, to declare His splendor and the richness of Christ that the whole world might come to know our Almighty Savior and be saved!

True worship is the total and yielding acceptance of the indwelling of God's Spirit within us from the crevices of our feet to the very follicles of our heads. It is the surrendering and outpouring of every ounce of our hearts and spirits in communion with Him in praise and worship and thanksgiving until we are completely spent- blocking all else that attempts to take preeminence. It is the indescribable emptying of ourselves to God in love, adoration, humility, reverence, and total submission for His goodness and mercy towards us.

Worshipping Christ in spirit and in truth as He desires involves: meekly presenting a repentant heart, communing with and being obedient to His Spirit, remaining faithful to the truth of His Word, serving others as we serve Christ, being committed to His cause by representing Christ and representing Christ to others, and offering our very lives as a living sacrifice to Him.

When we can truly worship Christ in the fullness of our capacity, then we will experience Him in a manner we cannot contain. The light of God will shine so brilliantly through us that it will burst out involuntarily for all others to see. When we begin to worship God fully in spirit and in truth, we will cause the whole world to bow to Him in reverence. We will cause all others to know what a mighty and omnipotent God we serve.

You were made to be a worshipper of the Almighty God. You were made to be a living epistle; a temple of the living God. You were made to be an ambassador for Christ. You were made to reflect the glories of God's kingdom while here on earth so that you might bear witness to the magnificence of Him and draw others to Jesus our Lord. *That* is our purpose. *That* is our life as believers and worshippers of God.

We must not sit and idly wait for Christ to return. We must live with the urgent realization that life is but a vapor, and the expectation that we have much work to do. James, the brother of Jesus, implores us to meditate on the urgency of our task and says- "… you do not know what will happen tomorrow." He then asks, "for what is your life? It is even a vapor that appears for a little time, and then vanishes away."[5] Therefore, we must work in haste. Christ says-"I must work the works of Him who sent Me while it is day; the night is coming when no one can work." (John 4:9)[6] We must emulate our Christ. Life was not given to us merely for our personal happiness and fulfillment. It was given to us that we might worship, serve and honor Jesus Christ our Lord. We have work to do!

We were made to worship God in the fullness and completeness of worship. God is calling you to worship Him as He desires. Will you answer and abide by His call?

Commitment time! Earlier you were asked to make a commitment to God. Right now, I want you to pray and then very specifically write what you will do for the kingdom of God going forward from this very moment. What will you do to ensure the glory of Christ's works will be passed on to the next generation? What will you commit to do to carry on the work of God?

_____

_____

_____

_____

_____

_____

_____

_____

Conclusion

~~~

L et us become true and authentic worshippers of Christ.
Don't be satisfied with just reading this book; apply
what you've read and the things you've penned to your life.
Become a doer, not just a hearer, of God's Word. Refer back
to your journal regularly to ensure you stay on track in your
spiritual growth. Then push yourself to grow even more.

Let us learn to worship Christ in the unity of His Spirit.
Let all of the redeemed of the Lord lift our hands and our
hearts in genuine worship. Let us lift our voices to wor-
ship the King of Kings. Let us bow before the holy name of
Christ. Let us sing in unison- We love you! We praise you!
We adore you!

We were made to worship! After all, God has done
too much for us not to worship Him. Even as the angels in

heaven now worship, let us worship and praise His name for ever, and forever, and forever more!

"Now to Him who is able to do exceedingly abundantly above all we ask or think, according to the power that works in us, to Him be glory in the church by Christ Jesus to all generations, forever and ever! Amen."[7]

Unto Him who is the only one worthy of all praise, all honor and all glory; to Him whom we raise our hands and our hearts in worship- our incredible, Almighty God. We worship you Father. We thank you for sending your Son- Jesus the Christ. We lift our hands to worship! We lift our voices to worship! We bow before Your holy name, for we were made to worship you!

—L

Prayer Reflection

What has God spoken to you in your prayers?

_____

_____

_____

_____

_____

_____

_____

_____

What did you say or promise to God?

_____

_____

_____

_____

_____

_____

_____

_____

Additional Notes and Reflections

_____

_____

_____

_____

_____

_____

_____

_____

_____

_____

_____

_____

_____

_____

_____

APPENDIX I

Made To Worship
Spiritual Gifts Assessment

∽∾

This assessment is designed to aid your journey to identify which gifts you have received of the Holy Spirit. It does not cover every spiritual gift. It will not give absolute evidence of your spirit-endowed gifting, but it will point to what your spiritual gift(s) might be. You may very likely have other gifts that will add to your unique God-given ability to serve His kingdom. True and full discovery of your gift(s) requires prayer, study, self-examination and putting your talents to work. Like any present, it is impossible to fully appreciate, understand or make effective use of your gift until it has been opened, explored, and used. Spiritual gifts are for kingdom building. They are given for the purpose of glorying God, continuing His work, and edifying His people. 1 Timothy 4:14 tells us to "neglect not the gift that is in thee". Therefore, as you complete this assessment, pray that God will reveal your gift(s) and illuminate how you can use them for His glory.

Instructions: Choose a response based on what most accurately describes you: 3= Definitely me; 2= Probably me; 1= Definitely _not_ me. For each statement, record the response number that most applies to you in the space provided.

1. I am able to coordinate people and resources to ensure a task is completed effectively.	
2. I feel compelled to share the Gospel of Christ and convert people to Christianity.	
3. I can generally sense when things are not quite what they appear to be.	
4. I like to tell others about Christ and do so every opportunity I get.	
5. I enjoy encouraging others who are discouraged and down-hearted.	
6. I am strongly confident that God will get me through both good and bad times.	
7. I give liberally of my time and money on a regular basis.	
8. I am greatly convicted to pray for healing and strongly believe in God's power to heal.	

9. I enjoy welcoming guests and helping them to feel at ease.	
10. I am able to read God's Word and easily translate how it relates to daily living.	
11. I am usually the one who decides how to get things done.	
12. I empathize with those who are embarrassed and belittled and seek to comfort them.	
13. I passionately speak with conviction and love what I believe God wants people to know.	
14. I like to talk with God constantly throughout the day.	
15. I always speak the truth with conviction even when difficult or challenging to do so.	
16. I enjoy volunteering to help whenever needed.	
17. I love to communicate biblical truths in such a way that it is easily understood by others.	
18. When a challenge is presented, I seek God's direction to identify a solution.	
19. When in a group, I like to ensure things are planned & organized as effectively as possible.	
20. I want to help the entire world hear the Gospel of Christ.	
21. I can often discern what is/is not of God when listening to those who claim to speak for him.	
22. I like to communicate the Gospel to non-believers in ways they can easily understand.	

23. I find that I am always trying to lift someone's spirit and share an encouraging word.	
24. I believe that whatever you ask for in prayer you will receive.	
25. I regularly give my money and belongings to those in need.	
26. I have a deep sense of compassion for the sick & pray specifically that God will heal them.	
27. I like having guests at my home.	
28. I have a burning desire to learn as much as I can about God's Word.	
29. I am good at setting goals & identifying directions a group should take to complete a task.	
30. When I see a person in need, I am driven to assist them.	
31. I am compelled to provide spiritual leadership to those seeking to know Christ.	
32. When I become aware of a need in a person's life, I instantly stop to pray for them.	
33. When God reveals a new insight in His Word, I am eager to immediately tell others.	
34. I don't mind doing the little jobs that others consider unimportant.	
35. I am able to express my thoughts in a manner to clearly present a Bible lesson to others.	
36. People often come to me for help in applying Christian faith & values to personal situations.	

37. I like handling details to ensure all items necessary to complete a task are done efficiently.	
38. I feel compelled to reach out to new individuals to invite them into relationship with Christ.	
39. I am certain of the Holy Spirit's presence in my life and in the lives of others.	
40. I find it easy to share with non-believers what Jesus Christ means to me.	
41. I like to encourage others through what I say.	
42. During a crisis, my trust in the Holy Spirit's presence is a source of strength for others.	
43. I cheerfully give my tithe and more to the work of the Lord.	
44. I completely trust that God can heal the sick & have evidenced their physical restoration.	
45. I am propelled to make all people feel included and accepted.	
46. I don't feel my day is complete without taking time to study & ponder over God's Word.	
47. I am a take charge person; I like to get things done.	
48. I have a very sympathetic heart towards those in need.	
49. I have a deep desire to share God's Word so that people know what He expects of them.	
50. I often become so absorbed in my prayer life that I block out all else around me.	

51. I often see a biblical truth that others fail to see & challenge others to respond to it.	
52. I look for ways to help others.	
53. I like to express my faith by assisting others discover the truths contained in the Bible.	
54. I often ask myself, what would God want me to do in this situation?	
55. I like to ensure that people are aware of the tasks needed to be done to complete a project.	
56. I enjoy sharing God's Word with people of different backgrounds and cultures.	
57. I am generally able to identify deceptive efforts to lead others away from Christ.	
58. I am constantly urged to invite others to church.	
59. I often challenge others to reach their full potential in Christ.	
60. I don't allow the pessimism of others to derail me even when things are not going well.	
61. I enjoy contributing to the needs of others.	
62. God uses my concerns & efforts as a means to heal the illnesses and disease of others.	
63. I take pleasure in meeting new people and becoming acquainted with them.	
64. My study of the Bible has proven helpful to others in their walk with Christ.	
65. I am able to guide and motivate people to join in the achievement of common goals.	

66. I feel an urgency to provide housing for the homeless and comfort for those in distress.	
67. I feel an obligation to provide spiritual guidance to an individual or group of believers.	
68. Believers often ask me to pray for them.	
69. I am often compelled to encourage others to repent & live according to God's commands.	
70. I like to help others so their work will be easier.	
71. People tell me I can make difficult ideas or biblical concepts more understandable.	
72. I regularly pray for insight as I ponder solutions that are best for me or others.	
73. I am very dependable for getting things done.	
74. I love to equip people to live faithful Christian lives.	
75. I have helped others determine whether their decisions were in accordance to God's Will.	
76. My goal is to help others become Christians.	
77. I am moved to help people who are experiencing conflicts or sorrow to feel better.	
78. I believe that God will do what seems impossible.	
79. I get a kick out of giving things away.	
80. People have often told me I have a healing touch or presence.	
81. When I see someone homeless on a cold night, I feel compelled to provide warm shelter.	

82. I can easily identify new insights & biblical truths and then share how it applies to our lives.	
83. People seem to respect me and follow my lead.	
84. I have a tender heart towards those in need and will often do what I can to help.	
85. People frequently come to me for spiritual help and guidance.	
86. I often pray for the salvation of non-believers.	
87. I courageously confront what is not of God & lovingly encourage a life lived for Christ.	
88. I find joy in serving others.	
89. I take time to diligently study God's Word so that I can accurately teach the Word of God.	
90. People often come to me with their personal problems for counsel.	

Now identify your spiritual gifts

Determine your probable, manifested spiritual gift(s) as follows:

☐ Place your response (1-3) in the blank next to the appropriate statement above.

☐ When completed, transfer your recorded answer to the corresponding space on the Identification Chart below.

☐ Tally the numbers from left to right and record them under "Total".

☐ If your total score is 10 – 15: there is strong evidence you may be blessed with this gift.

☐ If your total score is 6 - 9: God may be developing this gift in you.

☐ If you score 5 or below: your gift is most likely in another area.

Made to Worship Spiritual Gifts Identification Chart

Question number / Your Response					Total	Gift
1:	19.	37.	55.	73.		Administration
2.	20.	38.	56.	74.		Apostleship
3.	21.	39.	57.	75.		Discernment
4.	22.	40.	58.	76.		Evangelism
5.	23.	41.	59.	77.		Exhortation
6.	24.	42.	60.	78.		Faith
7.	25.	43.	61.	79.		Giving
8.	26.	44.	62.	80.		Healing
9.	27.	45.	63.	81.		Hospitality
10.	28.	46.	64.	82.		Knowledge
11.	29.	47.	65.	83.		Leadership
12.	30.	48.	66.	84.		Mercy
13.	31.	49.	67.	85.		Pastoring
14.	32.	50.	68.	86.		Prayer
15.	33.	51	69.	87.		Prophesy
16.	34.	52.	70.	88.		Serving/Helping
17.	35.	53.	71.	89.		Teaching
18.	36.	54.	72.	90.		Wisdom

What does my gift indicate, and how might it be used?

Administration – (1 Cor. 12:28) Persons with the gift of administration are generally take charge people; good at organizing people and resources to achieve a specific God-directed goal or purpose with great efficiency and success. Good with details, planning and organization, they are driven to ensure a group or organization works well together to accomplish a common goal. This gift can be used to provide church/auxiliary leadership, staffing, secretarial positions, etc. where organizational skills are important to ensure the efficient work of the body.

Apostleship – (1Cor. 12:28; Ephes. 4:11) Many with this gift have the desire to reach out and take the Gospel to new or unfamiliar communities, cultures, or territories. They enjoy sharing their faith and inviting others to develop a relationship with Christ. Some may become missionaries. Others may focus more on matters that pertain to church body leadership or maintaining authority over spiritual concerns relating to the church. This gift is valuable for outreach ministries within and beyond the church and community. This is extremely necessary in our efforts to "go ye therefore and make disciples..."

Discernment – (1Cor. 12:10; 1Cor.2:10-14) Provides persons the ability to clearly distinguish whether or not behavior, teachings, or other actions are of the Spirit of God. Discerning people have the ability to more easily separate God's truth from Satan's cloak of deception. They seek God's will and purpose and then apply that understanding to situations involving God's people. A great aid in our spiritual warfare to help ensure believers are not led astray.

Evangelism – (Ephes. 4:11) Persons with the gift of evangelism are eager messengers of God's Good News; willing to share the message of God to all to whom they avail themselves. Some may become preachers of the Gospel; others will share God's Word in more of a "laymen's" role. All are eager to get the Word of Christ to all who will listen. The gift of evangelism is critical in getting the Word of God out to the lost and non-believers.

Exhortation/Encouragement- (Romans 12:8) Exhibited in persons who naturally find themselves encouraging others;

helping others to maximize their potential through words of support and empowerment. They urge, warn, incite or encourage others towards a course of action. Exhorters help advise and awaken others to be all that God wants them to be; to build confidence; to comfort or console. A great gift in counseling, motivating, discipling, and working with others to positively build and grow the body of Christ.

Faith - (1 Cor. 12:8-10) This is more that the saving-belief in Jesus Christ. It is an over-riding, super-abundant confidence that God works all things together for the good of those called by the Lord; a staunch persuasion of God's power and His promises to accomplish His will; a deep, compelling, unshakable conviction that despite what you or others physically see with your eyes, you know and trust the power and plan of God. A must have in visionary leadership to guide followers in the direction God is leading even when they don't readily see it, and in a church's prayer ministries.

Giving – (Romans 12:8) Manifested in persons with a deep commitment to provide resources- such as time, money, or energy- as needed to support God's will and plan without any regard for what they'll receive in return. This gift is found in cheerful, generous persons who have a love for giving. These are great persons to assist with the material needs of the church and others in need. They may also be resourceful in identifying and cultivating donors and other resources for the needs of the church and others.

Healing – (1Cor. 12:9, 28) The gift through which God uses one to make others whole and healthy; the ability to channel God's healing love and comfort to help others grow sound either physically, emotionally, mentally or spiritually. While we most often think of doctors and other types of physicians, persons with this gift may also include counselors, pastors, and those with a gift of prayer. A very useful gift in healing those who are broken, hurting, and lost to become whole once again.

Hospitality – (Romans 12:13; 1 Peter 4:9) This gift affords persons the ability to willingly and ungrudgingly welcome and receive guests and those in need into their homes and into the house of the Lord. They openly extend a hand of love, warmth, and acceptance. A great gift that is useful for ushers, greeters, small group study hosts, welcoming center workers, New Member's mentors, and the general congregation to help receive others into the church.

Knowledge – (1Cor 12:8) Also noted as the Word of Knowledge; the speaking or sharing of insight received directly from God. It manifests as an insatiable desire to learn more of God and His Will for our lives and allows a deeper understanding of God's Word and how it converts, translates and applies to daily living. A needed gift for teachers within the church, spiritual advisers, Christian counselors, pastors and others who have the desire to help God's people live according to His Word.

Leadership [ruling/government] – (Romans 12:8; 1 Cor. 12:28) A system of ruling; leading or exercising authority over a organization. This gift enables one to give direction and guidance, and to motivate others to fulfill or complete God's work through various tasks or projects. Those with this gift are also take-charge type of people. A must have for any church or organization, persons with the gift of leadership serve well as officers, group or organizational leaders, staff, Sunday School superintendents, project leaders, etc.

Mercy – (Romans 12:8) The ability to cheerfully render compassion towards those in need and suffering, and then acts to meet that need. Persons with the gift of showing mercy have a forgiving, loving, and sympathetic disposition. Great persons to have on your social ministry teams, support groups, outreach programs, etc.

Pastoring – (Ephesians 4:11) Gives a believer the confidence, capability and desire to provide spiritual direction and leadership for individual or groups of believers. This gift does not always involve the office or position as a pastor of a church. The gift of pastoring, shepherding, or spiritual mentoring is valuable for small group or in-home Bible study leaders, children's, youth, young adult, or Vacation Bible School leaders, or other leaders of Christian discipleship.

Prayer – (Romans 12:12) Persons with this gift have an innate ability to intimately and earnestly talk with God, and are often very willing to do so on the behalf of others. Great persons to lead prayer services, to be prayer partners, help with the visitation of the sick and shut-ins, outreach, evangelism teams and other areas throughout the church.

Prophecy – (Romans 12:6; 1 Cor. 12:10, 28-29; Ephes. 4:11) The ability to be open to and used by God to offer deep, and many times foretelling insight and perspective through divine revelation. Persons with this gift are often compelled to speak forth the message of God to His people. Often found in pastors, evangelists, ministers and other clergy.

Service [helps/ministry]- (Romans 12:7; 1 Cor. 12:28; 1 Cor. 16:2-3; Ephes. 4:12) Enables a believer to gladly provide assistance to others; the God-given ability to submissively and humbly serve others. Often done behind the scenes, these persons are willing and eager to take care of the needs and help with the tasks of others. A wonderful gift that can be used throughout the church and beyond in all capacities. Persons with this gift serve from a sense of identity or calling, and seek opportunities to serve others as a way of serving God. These are your workers who serve with a heart of love.

Teaching – (Romans 12:7, 11; 1 Cor. 12:28; Ephes. 4:11) Persons with the gift of teaching have an innate ability to communicate knowledge and effortlessly help others learn. They can easily convey a personal understanding of the Bible and their faith in such a way that it is clear and straightforwardly understood by others. A very valuable gift in the development of God's people; required for all those working to edify God's people through His Word– Sunday School teachers, seminar leaders, Bible study teachers/leaders, Vacation Bible School, discipleship classes, etc.

Wisdom – (1 Cor. 2: 6-7; 1 Cor.12:8) The ability to speak the sound judgment of God as revealed by Him. It allows the believer to determine what is best for an individual believer or group of believers through a deeper understanding of God's Word. Persons with this gift are able to make biblical connections and to help others make biblical connections to understand the implications of their actions, behaviors and beliefs regarding the root causes of their conflicts, disagreements and barriers to spiritual growth. Often evidenced in pastors, spiritual advisors and other types of counselors, support group leaders, etc. A great gift in long-range planning, marital counseling, and other ministry teams.

Appendix II

Optional Group Discussion Questions

~~~

Day 1 Review– Welcome to the Kingdom

1. What prompted you to get involved in church? Did you wait for someone to ask you?

2. Why is it necessary for us to inwardly reflect on our spiritual lives and internally challenge ourselves to grow spiritually?

3. Why did you really join church initially?

4. What do you believe and what does that mean to you really?

5. What were some of your thoughts as you read and reflected on Day 1?

Day 2 Review – God's Great Love

1. When you reflect over your life, can you easily see where God protected you in spite of bad decisions and foolish living?

2. Without God's grace and His mercy, what do you think your life would be like at this point?

3. What would be your statement of witness as to what God has done for you and why you gave your life to Him?

Day 3 Review – A New Creation

1. How easily do you find yourself quickly judging someone else based on first impressions?

2. Is evaluating or examining "the fruit" someone bears the same as judging? Why or why not?

3. What does true conversion look like to you? How does this "new life" display itself on the outside? How does it play out?

4. What does Christ expect of you?

Day 4 Review – Growing in Christ

1. Why is growing in Christ a lifetime process?

2. Why must we be intentional in our spiritual growth?

3. Where did you rate yourself in your spiritual growth and why?

Day 5 Review – Made To Worship

1. Is worship a privilege or an obligation? Why?

2. The Holy Spirit will reveal God's Will for your life *if* you will allow God to speak to you. Why is the "if" important?

3. Doing God's Will begins when you start to envision God and His purpose for your life, and are open to allowing the Holy Spirit to teach you. What does that mean?

4. Why is our spiritual development directly related to the level of our commitment to God's purpose?

5. What were some of the things you listed/identified that you could do to learn God's will for your life that would give God continuous glory?

Day 6 Review – Authentic Worship

1. How would you define worship?

2. Why is it important to define and understand what authentic worship is?

3. Name some ways you can improve your relationship with God.

4. Any other comments regarding today's study?

Day 7 Review – Worshipping in Spirit

1. Scripture says- "God is Spirit and they that worship Him must worship Him in spirit and in truth." What does that mean to you?

2. Would your worship and your response to God be the same if no one was in the room but you?

3. Are your actions and utterances actually being directed to God?

Day 8 Review – Worshipping in truth

1. How do you view God?

2. What are your thoughts on the comment –"how you see or envision God and how you know Him influences how you worship Him". How might this impact how we praise and interact with God?

3. How can a more profound knowledge of Christ make you free to worship Him more abundantly?

4. How can relying on someone else's interpretation of God's Word get you in trouble?

Day 9 Review – God-centered Praise

1. Do we really rejoice in the Lord always?

2. Why is it so easy for us to focus on our problems vs. positively focusing on and praising God for all the blessings we either fail to recognize or simply take for granted?

3. What too easily captures your heart, eye, or attention and distracts you from your worship of God?

Day 10 Review –True Worship or Zealous Entertainment

1. What are you coming to church for?

2. How do our motives and intent impact our worship?

3. Do we truly direct all worship to God? How often do our songs or our worship focus on us versus pointing to and praising God?

4. How have we been guilty of using entertainment to draw attendees to church?

Day 11 Review – Make a Joyful Noise

1. How would you describe your praise? How do you think God would describe your praise?

2. Have you ever made judgments about someone else's worship? Why?

3. How can we ensure our worship is pleasing to God?

Day 12- Be Wary of Itching Ears

1. Why is it more important to have believers live out God's Word rather than *only* having leaders/preachers who effectively preach God's Word?

2. Why is mindless worship meaningless?

3. What are some things that you intentionally do to focus on how the word being preached specifically applies to you?

Day 13- Do We Reflect Christ?

1. Why are Christians so easily accused of being hypocrites?

2. How might we cause others to reject Christ?

3. Does your image on your days of worship align with your image during the rest of the week?

4. What do you think your lifestyle and behavior says about your worship?

5. If someone was to pronounce your eulogy tomorrow, would your ways and your lifestyle reflect the attributes of Christ?

Day 14- Worshipping Through Service

1. All of us value and protect our personal time, but why is it so difficult to sacrifice for the service of Christ?

2. What outward evidence shows that you love God?

3. Why do we sometimes find it difficult to serve others?

Day 15- Knowing and Using Your Spiritual Gifts

1. Do you know and are you using your spiritual gifts?

2. Why is it important to do so?

3. Can we select what spiritual gifts we prefer to have?

4. How might a spiritual gift be misused?

5. How can spiritual gifts help us work more effectively as a unified body in Christ?

Day 16 – A Living Sacrifice

1. What does "presenting your body as a living sacrifice" mean to you?

2. How often are you like Paul in the struggle of bringing your flesh into obedience to the will of God? Why?

3. What thoughts, attitudes, actions or lifestyle behaviors hinder you from daily committing your bodies and resources to God for His use?

4. What priorities could you change to provide the time and resources for you to do God's work?

Day 17- Being Doers of God's Word

1. Why is being submissive to God such a challenge for us?
2. What does James 1:22-23 say specifically to you? Why do we so easily forget our true image?
3. What must we do to remain "qualified to perform effective ministry"?
4. What impedes you from being a doer of God's Word and performing effective ministry?
5. What steps can you take to become a more effective worker for Christ?

Day 18 – Being Committed

1. Do you eagerly and genuinely welcome visitors into God's house?
2. Do you help set the tone and atmosphere that encourages them to come back and to seek to find you again?
3. Are you willing to make a commitment to a cause greater than yourself?

Day 19 – Called to Make a Difference

1. How do you show you were called to make a difference?

2. What must you fight to put aside in order to be effective disciple of Christ?

3. What difference can you make in the lives of those around you to help lead them to Christ?

Day 20 – Mirroring Great Worshippers

1. Would Christ consider you a "fair-weather" worshipper?

2. How do you react to adversity? Are you a carrot, an egg or a coffee bean?

3. How might a position, title, or place of attention cause you to think more highly of yourself than you should?

4. How might you become more like Job? David? Mary? or John the Baptist?

Day 21 – Infinite Worship

1. What will you do to ensure that the knowledge and glory of Christ will be passed on to the next generation?

2. What will you commit to do to carry on the work of Christ?

Endnotes

~~~

Introduction

1. Ephesians 1: 5-6,12 (NIV)

Day 2 – God's Great Love

1. John 14: 2-3 (NIV)

2. Ephesians 2: 4-10 (NIV)

3. Galatians 3: 26-29 (NIV)

4. Malachi 2:10 (NKJV)

5. 1 Corinthians 8:5-6

6. Ephesians 4: 4-6

7. Revelations 5: 9 (KJV)

8. Romans 10: 8-9 (NIV)

Day 3 – A New Creation

1. 2 Corinthians 5: 17 (NKJV)

2. Titus 3:5 (NIV)

Day 4 – Growing in Christ

1. Psalm 86: 11 (KJV)

2. Ephesians 4: 13-15 (NIV)

Day 5 – Made to Worship

1. Warren, R. (2008). 4th ed. Better Together: What on earth are we here for? (Introduction). Lake Forest, CA: Saddleback Church

2. Mark 12: 30 (NIV)

3. Williams, M. (2007). Made to Worship. Flow Records, Dallas/Ft. Worth.

4. John 6: 39-40 (NIV)

5. Numbers 23: 26 (NIV)

6. Willis, A.T.; Moore, K. (1996). Master Life- The Disciple's Personality, Book 2, (p11). Nashville, TN: Lifeway Press

7. Philippians 2: 13 (NIV)

8. John 4: 34 (NIV)

Day 6 – Authentic Worship

1. Temple, W. (1955). Readings in St. John's Gospel, Macmillian ed. London

2. Block, D. (n.d.). For the Glory of God course notes as posted by Bob Kauflin. Retrieved from http://www. worshipmatters.com/2005011/04/defining-worship/

3. Deffinbaugh, B. (1995). Worship, Part I, John 4: 1-26; Definition of Worship. Retrieved August 2010 from bible.org at http://bible.org/series;age/worship-part-1-john-41-26

4. Romans 11: 36 (KJV)

5. John 17:11 (KJV)

6. John 17: 17, 19 (KJV)

7. Deffinbaugh, B. (1995). Worship, Part I, John 4: 1-26;Further Light on Worship. Retrieved August 2010 from bible.org at http://bible.org/series;age/worship-part-1-john-41-26

8. Mark 12: 30 (NIV)

9. Hebrews 11: 6 (NKJV)

10. Psalm 9:1 (KJV)

Day 7 – Worshipping in Spirit

1. Simpson, S. (2005). The Biblical Definition of Worship. Retrieved August 2010 from the Apologetics Coordination Team website; http://wwwdeception-inthe church.com/biblicalworship.html

2. Psalm 29: 2 (KJV)

3. John 4: 24 (NKJV)

4. Warren, R. (2002). The Purpose Driven Life: What on Earth Am I Here For? (p.101). Grand Rapids, MI: Zondervan

5. 1 Corinthians 6: 20 (NKJV)

6. 1 Peter 1: 13-16 (NIV)

7. Hebrews 10: 25 (KJV)

8. John 4: 24 (NIV)

Day 8 – Worshipping in Truth

1. John 1:17b (NIV)

2. 1 Corinthians 2:1, 4-5 (NIV)

3. 2 Timothy 2: 15 (KJV)

4. Stanley, C. (1985). How to Listen To God (pp126 – 127). Nashville: Thomas Nelson, Inc.

5. Stanley, C. (1985). How to Listen To God (p77). Nashville: Thomas Nelson, Inc.

6. John 8:32 (NKJV)

7. John 14: 6 (NIV)

Day 9 – God-centered Praise

1. Psalm 22: 25 (NJKV)

2. Philippians 3: 20 (NIV)

3. Philippians 4:4 (NJKV)

4. Matthew 15:8 (NIV)

Day 10 – True Worship or Zealous Entertainment?

1. Psalm 33: 1,3 (NIV)

2. Psalm 47:1 (NIV)

3. Psalm 98:4,6 (NIV)

4. Exodus 34: 114 (KJV)

5. 1 Chronicles 15: 25- 29 (KJV)

Day 11 – Make A Joyful Noise

1. Psalm 81: 1 (KJV)

2. Psalm 149: 3 (KJV)

3. Psalm 150:5 (NKJV)

4. Psalm 150: 6 (NKJV)

5. Luke 19: 40 (NIV)

6. The Life Application Bible commentators (1991). Life Application Bible, New International Version Bible (p.689). Wheaton, Illinois: Tyndale House Publishers

7. 1 Chronicles 13: 8-10 (NIV)

Day 12- Be Wary of Itching Ears

1. Life Application Bible commentators (1991). Life Application Bible, New International Version (p.2208). Wheaton, IL: Tyndale House Publishers

2. Life Application Bible commentators (1991). Life Application Bible, New International Version (p.2208). Wheaton, IL: Tyndale House Publishers

3. Proverbs 14: 25 (NIV)

4. 1 Corinthians 14: 14-15 (NIV)

5. Acts 17: 11 (NIV)

6. Psalm 81: 8,11,13 (NIV)

7. 2 Timothy 4:3 (NIV)

Day 13- Do We Reflect Christ?

1. Ephesians 5: 15 – 17 (NIV)

2. Romans 3:23 (NIV)

3. 1 Corinthians 4:5b (NIV)

4. Galatians 5:22 (NIV)

5. Ephesians 4:1 (NIV)

6. Colossians 3:5 (NIV)

7. Colossians 3:9-10 (NIV)

8. 2 Peter 1: 5-8 (NIV)

9. Matthew 5: 14, 16 (NIV)

Day 14 – Worshipping Through Service

1. Hebrews 12:28 (KJV)

2. John 12:26 (KJV)

3. Luke 4:8 (NIV)

4. John 4:34 (NKJV)

5. John 14: 12 (NIV)

6. James 1:22 (NIV)

7. Matthew 28: 19-20 (NIV)

8. Deuteronomy 10: 12 (NIV)

9. John 17:18 (NIV)

10. 1 Corinthians 13: 1-3 (NIV)

11. Psalm 116: 12 (NKJV)

12. Matthew 20:28 (NIV)

13. Galatians 5:13 (NIV)

14. Colossians 3: 23-24 (NIV)

15. 1 Peter 4: 11 (NIV)

Day 15- Knowing and Using Your Gifts

1. Romans 12:6 (NIV)

2. Romans 12:11-13 (NIV)

3. 1 Corinthians 13:2 (NIV)

4. Ephesians 4:12-13 (KJV)

5. Zaspel, F. (1996). Definitions or What is a Spiritual Gift? (Chapt.1). Word of Life Baptist Church Website. Retrieved Feb. 2010 from http://www.biblicalstudies.com/bstudy/spirituagifts/ch01.htm

6. Zaspel, F. (1996). Definitions or What is a Spiritual Gift? (Chapt.1). Word of Life Baptist Church

Website. Retrieved Feb. 2010 from http://www.bibli-calstudies.com/bstudy/spirituagifts/ch01.htm

7. 1Corinthians 12: 4-6 (NKJV)

8. Rogers, A. (2007). What Every Christian Ought to Know Day By Day (p297). Nashville: B& H Publishing Group

9. 1 Corinthians 12:7 (NIV)

10. 1 Corinthians 12:31 (NKJV)

11. Rogers, A. (2007). What Every Christian Ought to Know Day By Day (p316). Nashville: B& H Publishing Group

Day 16 – A Living Sacrifice

1. Romans 6:2 (NIV)

2. Romans 6:4 (NIV)

3. Romans 6:11-13 (NIV)

4. Life Application Bible commentators (1991). Life Application Bible, New International Version (p.2050). Wheaton, IL: Tyndale House Publishers

5. Life Application Bible commentators (1991). Life Application Bible, New International Version (p.2050). Wheaton, IL: Tyndale House Publishers

6. Romans 7:18-23

7. Mark 11:24 (NIV)

Day 17- Being Doers of God's Word

1. James 1: 22-24 (NIV)

2. 1 Corinthians 15:58 (KJV)

3. John 15:5 (KJV)

4. Life Application Bible commentators (1991). Life Application Bible, New International Version (p1913). Wheaton, IL: Tyndale House Publishers

5. John 15:6 (NIV)

6. Ephesians 5:18 (NIV)

7. 2 Timothy 4:7 (NIV)

Day 18 – Being Committed

1. Luke 9:23 (KJV)

2. Malachi 3:6a (KJV)

3. 2 Cor. 9:7(NIV)

Day 19- Called to Make a Difference

1. Matthew 28: 19-20 (KJV)

2. Psalm 121:1-2 (KJV)

3. Psalm 121:3,5,7-8 (NIV)

4. Mark 9:23 (NKJV)

5. Hebrews 12:1 (KJV)

6. Hebrews 12:1 (NIV)

7. 2 Timothy 1:6 (KJV)

8. Philippians 3:14 (NIV)

9. Matthew 9:37 (NIV)

Day 20 – Mirroring Great Worshippers

1. Job 1:21 (KJV)

2. Exodus 20:20 (KJV)

3. Psalm 1:3 (NIV)

4. Romans 12:3 (KJV)

5. James 1:17 (NIV)

6. 1 Chronicles 22:19a (NIV)

7. 1 Chronicles 16:8-12 (NIV)

8. Luke 10:42 (NKJV)

9. Psalm 139:23 (NIV)

10. John 1: 15, 32 (NKJV)

11. Acts 19:4 (NKJV)

12. Romans 12:2 (KJV)

Day 21 – Infinite Worship

1. Psalm 146:2 (NIV)

2. Psalm 145:2 (NKJV)

3. Psalm 145:47; 10-12

4. Psalm 145:21 (KJV)

5. James 4:14 (NKJV)

6. John 9:4 (NKJV)

7. Ephesians 3:20-21(NKJV)

CPSIA information can be obtained at www.ICGtesting.com
Printed in the USA
LVOW081352201011

251371LV00002B/11/P